Keep On Believing

Stories of Inspiration, Courage, and Triumph

by John Seeley M.A.

Published by Heart Fire Press

EDITORIAL OFFICE:
Blue Moon Wonders
4492 Camino de la Plaza Suite 564
San Diego, CA 92173

Editorial and production: Bob Adams
Type design and typography: Sam Johnson
Formatting by Claudia Suzanne
Cover design: Karen Floyd, San Diego, CA
Cover photo By Larry Silva, c. 2014

Library of Congress Cataloguing-in-Publication Data

Seeley, John Herbert.
Keep On Believing / John Herbert Seeley

ISBN: 978-0976594239
Printed in the USA on acid-free paper
Distributed by Blue Moon Wonders

10 9 8 7 6 5 4 3 2 1

Manufactured in the United States
First Edition

Table of Contents

Dedication

To all the people that are unemployed, underemployed, or feeling stuck and uninspired, this book is for you. It is my hope to reignite the passion for life, and motivate you to follow your dreams. Use these stories for inspiration to lift your vision for what is possible and then take the first step toward creating the life you really want. You can if you believe you can!

Acknowledgments

I want to thank Ron and Mary Hulnick and the University of Santa Monica for teaching the Master's Program in Spiritual Psychology. I want to especially thank all the contributing authors, alumni of the University of Santa Monica: Dominique Lelong, Susan Ortolano, Anna Huckabee Tull, Thury Byrkett, Nancy Burcham, Maryellen Bein, Teresa McKee, Laurel Airica, David Cooper, Linda Luke, Dayna Dunbar, Dr. Jeanne Michele, Jennifer Rose Aronson, Joelene Robinson, Victoria Koutavas, Anne-Marie Arrow, Nancy Gex Klifman, Deirdre Pasky, Donna Edwards Goldman, M.A, Judi Larson, Jeff Youngs, Ivana Siska, Beverly Lubin and Alexia Roberts.

I want to also thank Karen Floyd for her beautiful cover design.

I want to thank my brother Michael Seeley, my sisters Janet Matte, Mary Baker, my brother-in-law Gene Baker, my brother-in-law Jack Wolowiec, my niece Jill Lucchesi, my nephew Jason Lucchesi, my grand nieces Cassandra Matte and Victoria Lucchesi, and my grand nephew Alex Lucchesi for their support.

Thanks also to my good friends Larry Silva, Tom and Mary Jo Malone, Amanda van der Gulik, Rob van der Gulik, Melissa Stewart, Doug and Valorie Knowlton, Rhonda and Phillippe Berckmans, Jeff and Anna Simmert, Amy Simmert, Kevin and Gail Slowik, Jim and Sandy Greunke, Wil Winkle, Steve and Gail Schmidbauer, Ed and Mary Lynn Seybold, John O'Connor, Simone Dean, Melvin and Sherrie Allen, Thelene Scarborough, Joanne Shales, Luis Turolla, Lynda Dyer, Glen Ledwell, Natalie Ledwell, Ryan Higgins, Eli Davidson, Raymond Powers, Maggie Carias, Nataliya Nozharova, Laura Meyers, Lynlae Sterllayn, Leslie Smith, Doug Rye and Anna Zimmerman, John and Julie Giljam, Molly Post and Arthur Kanegis, Randy Seol, Hugo Ramirez, Kris Franks, Zach Perlman, Rose Baush, Peter Burt, Steve Perry and Journey for their support and inspiration!

Introduction

I Was Sunk By the Coast Guard!

by John Seeley M.A.

There is no better than adversity. Every defeat, every heartbreak, every loss, contains its own seed, its own lesson on how to improve your performance the next time." --Malcolm X

My life has offered me numerous chances to quit and to just give up. I certainly have had moments where I seriously considered it. Plato said you're either growing or decaying. I've done a bit of both, and it is an ongoing process for me.

I wrote in my first book about my "worst year." The year involved me getting fired three times; then my best friend committed suicide, and I found him. Then my dog died, my fiancée left me and I got fired yet again. I was seriously depressed and got no help. So the depression just ran my life for almost a decade.

When I say it ran my life, I mean that I chose not to get help. I didn't know any better; like many people, I thought, "I just have to tough it out." Yet I had no skills or help to figure out how to heal from life's traumas. If you only react to life, you are at its mercy. Luckily, I discovered I have a choice and by being proactive, I can make things much better.

I now realize that my world was a reflection of my unresolved issues. Life was offering me the chance to "see" what I was feeling; the results I got reflected the pain and guilt I felt inside.

In the "bad decade" that followed, I experienced losing my best friend, my fiancée, my father, my wife and finally my mom. Finally, all of the pain from losing everyone all came up and I could no longer function. This was my tipping point to shift my life. This began my journey into reinventing who I was. I began attending counseling sessions and personal growth workshops. I was reading five self-help books each week.

I began to see the world in a new light. I was remembering the confident person I had been in my early twenties. From the workshops, books and counseling, I saw a bigger vision than I ever thought possible. Life was getting better. I was learning things about myself and life. I attended numerous personal development workshops and even staffed many of them, too. I had no reason to at the time, but I saw myself as a facilitator of this work.

I went back to graduate school again, this time for Spiritual Psychology. On the day after my graduation, the company I worked for determined that I would be better off working elsewhere. The way I saw it, I was ready for a new chapter of my life and the Universe was assisting the transition. I began working on my first book right then. That lead me to the "I was Sunk by the Coast Guard" story, and this *Keep On Believing* concept.

To promote my first book, *Get Unstuck! The Simple Guide to Restart Your Life,* I came up with the idea of using the world's only amphibious RV as the vehicle that never gets stuck, to gain attention. To maximize the exposure, I thought we should take it to the biggest media event, the Super Bowl. We took it to Jacksonville in 2005 to do just that.

It was pouring rain for two straight weeks before the game, and we couldn't do the promotion to get the PR we wanted the week before the game. I proposed that we host a party on the RV during the game with celebrities and cheerleaders to give a reason for additional TV coverage. FOX, who was broadcasting the game, agreed it was a good idea. We began rounding up celebrities. That was on Tuesday before the game.

On Wednesday we informed the Coast Guard that we would be having more people on the RV, and they responded that they would now consider us a commercial vehicle. That required a Certified Ship's Captain on board. I relayed that information to the RV folks, and the builder said that he had been a Certified Ship's Captain, but his license had expired due to his mom being ill, and not having the chance to renew it. He said he knew the head of the Coast Guard in that area, and perhaps he could have a word with him to see if we could work something out. I said okay, and the next day we would look for a launch site, and maybe a Ship's Captain too.

On Thursday we found the perfect site and we found a boat at the dock with a couple of guys on it. I asked them if they knew a Certified Ship's Captain who might like to be on the RV in the Super Bowl. One guy responded that he was one, and would do that for free! Now we were all set!!

The next day the weather was scheduled to be sunny for the first time in two weeks. We had three camera crews meeting us at 10am. I went back to my hotel in great spirits. A couple hours later, I got a call from my PR guy. He got a call from the RV folks, and they had word from the Coast Guard.

It began with "We have enough trouble keeping these waterways safe without you." I knew it wasn't good news after that. It continued, "We did some checking, and that RV is not registered as a boat. Therefore you cannot put that it in the waters in the State of Florida."

I suggested we go to a river in Georgia 40 miles away and shoot B-roll footage, then park the RV next to the stadium and film more there. When we pitched the idea to FOX, they said, "If we can't shoot from the RV in the water with Jacksonville in the background, we don't care!" That was it. Everything was over. We were sunk! I felt like I had been hit in the gut!

The next morning I woke up with the Journey song, "Don't Stop Believin'" in my head. I took it as a good sign, and then thought it would make a good book title. When I was watching the game I saw a FedEx commercial that featured Journey's "Don't Stop Believin'" song again. It was yet another sign for me to pursue my dream and bring my message to the world. Later I realized the title was a negative affirmation, so I changed it to "Keep On Believing," and presto, here's the result. I even wrote a "Keep On Believing" song as our anthem.

The stories in this book are about overcoming the challenges of life, persevering through tough times, and following dreams to find a life of fulfillment and love. Each author takes you through their struggle, and shows you how they triumphed over self doubt, depression, stress and feeling lost.

I continue to have challenges, as we all do. I just know that I can find my way out, and I do it a whole lot faster than I used to. Keep reading and I hope these stories inspire you in your life.

Know that you are not alone in your challenge and that others have found a pathway out. You can too! Please pay it forward and pass the word so that others to be inspired too. Then look for us at the Super Bowl. We'll be the ones singing "Keep On Believing" in the water~!

Footsteps

by Dominique Lelong

*"Let me walk three weeks in the footsteps of my
enemy, carry the same burden, have the same trials
as he, before I say one word to criticize."*
--Dale Carnegie

Have you ever stepped into someone else's shoes?
I did. One day I saw an abandoned pair and
with some hesitation, I stepped inside of them.
They felt too big for my little feet but no one seemed
to notice.
As I kept on walking they were more and more eager
to show me where to go.
I needed them and they needed me to feel alive.
When I was losing myself, they were helping me to
find my way;
when I was falling they were raising me up taller than
ever;
when I was too tired to go on they carried me on;
where I had to show up for myself,
where I had to show up for others,
where I had to show up in the background of
my faded desires, my faded hopes, my faded courage.
It is not easy to fill in for someone else's presence,
for someone else's expectations, for someone else's
footsteps.
It is hard to keep on moving forward
when the wind bends everything up and down;
it is hard to keep on moving forward
when the glare of the sun blindfolds one's destination.
It is hard to keep on moving forward
when the moon does not show up for a chance to rest;

it is hard to keep on moving forward
when the rain goes sideways, hurting one's face along
the way.
Who can say that one life is more difficult than
another one?
But I was an expert at comparing at the heart of my
frozen wounds.
The kaleidoscope of all emotions is the same,
I believe it all depends how we hold on to them.
One day as I was putting on the shoes,
I had this strange feeling;
I was now a stranger to myself.
Looking around,
I woke up in a new reality.
As I took a step forward
the bottom of the shoes separated themselves.
There was a deep broken bond;
there was no glue to hold us tight together anymore.
They looked exhausted, their job seemed to be done
and my attachments for them had transformed.
I felt it at all levels of my being.
So just like that, I abandoned them...
in need of being repaired,
in need of loving care,
in need of wanting me
to keep on needing them.
There was no going back.
I had moved on.
To this day, I cherish – for better and for worse – all
my memories with this pair of shoes.
I have to admit, they were never mine to begin with,
but they showed me the way home to myself.
It was now time for me
to find my own to fill,
my own to own,
my own to take me back
where I now belong in my life.

Since then I have owned many pairs,
each unique in their unlimited ways,
to show me where I have to go.
I have to say that it feels good
to stand up on my own two feet,
at peace with myself,
even on shaking ground.
I do not have to pretend anymore
to be someone else,
I do not have to pretend
to act beyond my will,
I do not have to pretend
to be stuck in a rut on a map made for me.
I have walked so far in my life to return to me,
finding beauty through all the seasons of my heart.
Reflecting back,
I know that all these years were not wasted,
as they have held the key for me
to find my way to be set free.
It is a good thing
that we do not know what tomorrow will bring,
as I have played God enough in my life
while stepping into someone else's shoes,
who had played God one day;
to choose to stop walking
by abandoning the gift of a life
worth living, in the eyes of a soul.
Forgiveness, compassion, gratitude is all there is.
There is only love at the beginning,
there is only love at the heart of all,
there is only love at the end of it all,
to carry someone else like me
with a large hole in her shoes
inviting a precious life to surrender while being
unfolded.

Dominique's Take-Away "This poem is a journey of transformation which goes through a sacred circle of empathy, forgiveness, compassion and gratitude, centering on the expression of love at the heart of it all. The lesson of this poem is that while my life brought many challenges, I learned to attune and trust in order to keep my heart open to see the gifts through all of my life's experiences. This spiritual pathway of humbleness helped me to find my way back home to my authentic self."

Losing A Friend and Finding Myself

by John Seeley M.A.

"When you make the finding yourself - even if you're the last person on Earth to see the light - you'll never forget it."--Carl Sagan

I met Bob through a mutual friend I'd known since freshman year at high school. Bob and I grew to be best friends through my high school and college years. Once when we were 17, my friends Tom, Bob and I took a trip to Canada. We were driving across the border, and the Canadian Border Patrol stopped us and asked us how much money we had. Bob responded, "What's it to you?" So for the next hour we enjoyed them tearing apart my car to make sure we were not smuggling anything. So you see, Bob was a bit of a smart-ass.

After college, I got a job and began my professional life. After eight months, the company was sold and I was laid off. I took advantage of the time off to travel and look for jobs elsewhere, including Knoxville, TN, at the World's Fair, and in New York City. Bob came along and we drove a lot that year. He had become a truck driver to support his wife and daughter, but then he'd been laid off from his job, too. He was planning on returning to college, but that was not to be.

I had moved to Madison, WI, and enrolled in a graduate school of business. I met a beautiful dental hygienist. As I was looking at her eyes while she was cleaning my teeth, my heart just opened up like never before. I fell for her immediately. We started dating and I knew I wanted to marry her. I knew I needed to get another job so I could do that, so I began working for my fiancée's father. This was doomed from the beginning. The existing manager realized that I was being groomed to replace him, since the restaurant was losing a lot of money, when it should have been profitable. So the manager set me up. The owner didn't like tap beer, but the manager didn't tell me, and then he let me put it in anyway. Then the manager told the owner I'd done it against his wishes.

Although the owner was an astute businessman, he didn't like anyone standing up to him. He took me out into the middle of the dining room and chewed me out. I was fuming! He tried to humiliate me in front of the customers! Had I not been in love with his daughter, I would have told him off in no uncertain terms. Why he chose to believe the manager, who had proven to be stealing from him, and do that to me, was shocking.

In a few months I turned the restaurant around, but the personality conflict between us resulted in my leaving. Once again I was unemployed. This, and my fiancée's parents, put pressure on my relationship with their daughter. I began looking for another job, this time in Chicago. During this time, my friend Bob had been going through his own turmoil. His marriage had broken down and he was going through the process of divorce. I used to say, "Life sucks, but it beats the alternative." Bob's response was, "I'm not so sure."

About two weeks had passed since I had said that, and I invited Bob to come to Chicago for my last interview before getting a job offer. He said no, and that he'd see me when I got back in a few days. That was Monday. On Wednesday I got a call from Bob's mom, asking if I knew where he was. I told her no, but I would be back the next day. I went back to Milwaukee and started looking where I thought Bob might be. When I got to his sister's house, I had a bad feeling. The smell of gas was unmistakable. As I entered the house my heart was pounding. I was feeling the worst possibility was true. As I walked into the kitchen I found Bob, dead. The gas had been on for two days and I'm lucky I didn't spark anything. I heard the fire trucks approach as I walked out. I identified Bob, so his family wouldn't have to. I went into shock. I was functioning, but almost like a robot. I didn't know what to do or what to feel, so I shut down my feelings just to survive.

I had some other friends who had also committed suicide over the years, but Bob's death hit me really hard. I thought I knew him. I never suspected that he might take his own life. We were so close and I had no clue he was upset! I felt that if he could do that, what else have I been wrong about? I wondered why he would leave. He had so much going for him. Why would he leave me? Why would he not tell me he was so upset? Why didn't I know?

From then on, my world spun out of control. I became very depressed. No one in my family knew what to do. I didn't know what to do. I cried a lot. Right after that, my dog died. Slowly I moved on, but being defensive put too much stress on an already pressured relationship, and my fiancée left me. After a few months at the new job, again due to my defensiveness, I lost that too.

I cried when I was told I was being fired. I knew that losing that last job, was the nail in the coffin of my relationship with my ex-finance. I finally realized that I would be better off not working for someone else, so I decided to buy my own restaurant. That seemed like the answer.

Unfortunately, there was a grain boycott to Russia. Farmers suffered a big downturn, and so did the mile-long farm tractor factory across the street, which had been in business for 100 years! It went bankrupt! Most of my customers worked for that factory, so I had a very hard time in my business. I worked 100 plus hours a week, and still made almost nothing. Some months I even lost money! I could have worked and McDonald's as a fry cook and made a lot more money and had less stress. I almost wish I had.

Why me? I wondered why I was suffering so much. Why was all this happening to me? What more could go wrong? I soon found out. After struggling for four years, I finally decided to get out of the restaurant business. I went back to graduate business school, and put the restaurant for sale.

The building's owner had had a big "For Sale" sign on the building for the past year, which didn't help business. He convinced me to tear up the lease so we could sell the two as a package and then get more for both. Once I did, he sold the building and I received a 30 day notice to move my restaurant.

With no time to sell the "business," I sold the equipment on the final day that I was open. I received a down payment, but I never received another payment. So I had to take another restaurant job in Chicago to pay off my bills from my restaurant. After a year and a half there, I paid them off and then got fired again!

I didn't know it then, but I was being prepared for my future career. I didn't realize that my outer world was a reflection of my inner one. I felt anger and guilt around Bob's death, and I created my own punishment in the form of demanding jobs and unfair terminations.

It was during my decade of undiagnosed depression that I got married. My depression culminated when my parents died within 3 years of each other, and I got divorced. I finally felt so overwhelmed that I reached out for professional help. After some trial and error, I found a good therapist and also went to personal development workshops. I began recovering. I started reading five self-help books a week. I read books like *You Can Heal Your Life, The Road Less Traveled, Think and Grow Rich, Care of the Soul*, and many more.

I found the passion to heal. I continued learning and growing and began to break free. I joined groups that embraced healing and growth. I went back to graduate school, this time for psychology, instead of business. Each step brought me more clarity about myself, healing, and how life works.

I never knew that I had my own PTSD from Bob's death. I never suspected it would affect me and my behavior for years. I felt like a victim. I felt I had no control. Everything was happening to me! I didn't know how I was creating this in my life.

My understanding of life was so limited then. I know now it's a life-long journey of learning and growing, and my confidence has been rebuilding to be able to risk again. It wasn't until I took some responsibility about my life that I was able to feel empowered again. Even though I don't have control over what happens around me, I do have the choice of deciding how I respond to life. That gives me power in my world and in my life.

Now I have been on a path to teach others how to break free of their blocks that have kept them from creating the life they truly desire. Even now, I have had times of struggle, and knowing how to shift isn't always enough. I find that creating support of friends, family, and professionals gives me the courage and strength to work through the challenges life still offers me. Life is a dance with steps forward and back, side to side and sometimes spinning around. I keep moving and rebalancing to the music of life. Life takes skill and perseverance, and is both a challenge and a joy.

I don't pretend to know everything about life. What I do know is that I am learning each day. I am given a new chance to grow and learn from each moment. Sometimes I succeed, and sometimes I still fail. I learned that it's okay to fail. In fact through failure, you learn, or at least have the opportunity to, if you are willing.

I have learned to heal the relationships I have with God, with women and most of all with myself. I learned to trust again. I learned that I will be okay no matter what happens around me.

I never could have predicted my life even 30 years ago, but it is far from dull. Now I am committed to help others to get through their challenges and to see them as opportunities for growth and development. If you can see the opportunity, you will find the lesson and be one step closer to enlightenment. That is how you transform tragedy to triumph! Keep On Believing!

John's Take-Away "I realize that I am creating my reality and how I feel about myself inside is reflected to me in my world. That gives me the power to make my life what I really want it to be."

The Quest for True Love

by Susan Ortolano, M.A. PCC, CMRC

"And think not you can direct the course of love, for love, if it finds you worthy, directs your course."
--Khalil Gibran

There I was, 33 years old, signing divorce papers after 8 years of what felt like a nasty prison sentence. Although we were married for just over 5 of them, I considered it a relationship train wreck.

As I sat there staring at my soon to be ex - husband, perplexed as to why I married him, I remembered ignoring the blazing "red flags" glaring at me while we were initially dating. And even though I could feel a deep sigh of relief, I began to wonder about my future and if I would ever find real love.

I'll admit I was carrying a boatload of wicked judgments about the eight mostly miserable years of the relationship I had chosen. Of course, most of those judgments were all about him. And, while I felt I was walking away with my head held high, having honored the wedding vows we originally made, I was immersed in a vat of victimhood, feeling like he'd been the one who had "done me wrong."

I'd spent most of those painful years walking on very sharp, prickly egg shells, living in constant fear, as my then-husband consistently made up bizarre stories about his whereabouts. He would often disappear at all hours of the day and night and I never knew where he *really* was, nor did I honestly believe his poorly-constructed explanations. There were no cell phones as it was the age of "pagers," so all I could do was page him and page him and page him, but he wouldn't call.

The truth is that he lied, and cheated with other women several times over and finally got caught. Ouch! His final "parting gift" to me towards the end was a whopper of an STD, proving to me that I was making the right decision to end the marriage. Good thing the STD was curable.

There is so much more to the story that would cause anyone's eyes to bulge and mouth to drop open. But the point is, I had been married to a man who lied, cheated, left me to pay for most everything as he didn't always feel like working, was obsessed with photographing naked women, soliciting my friends and anyone one else he could get to pose, and ultimately treated me like the naive mother of a rebellious, horny, badly-behaved teenager, constantly draining the life force out of me.

While I was relieved to be moving on, I was well aware that I had some major reflecting to do. Being treated like that in the marriage had rocked my feelings of self-worth and esteem to the core, bringing up a lot of despair and rage, along with a large dose of self-doubt that had me even question my sense of value. I also must admit, it hadn't been the first time I had been with a man who had treated me poorly, cheated, and lied, and I certainly wanted it to be the last.

I felt very dazed and confused with my experiences in the world of relationships. I certainly had dated some kinder men, who just weren't quite right, but had to recognize that there had been a "pattern" of similar experiences and knew I had to make some changes. I deeply understood the importance of having a loving relationship in my life and had a strong desire to be a happily married woman.

So, how did I go from being married to a man who lied, cheated, and treated me like dirt to finding and marrying the man of my dreams? First, I had what I call a "Scarlet O'Hara" moment. I had immersed myself into some spiritual and personal growth programs and made a critical declaration. I declared that I would rather be single for the rest of my life than settle for someone who wasn't right for me. I decided I'd never settle or sacrifice myself again.

Then, I faced that similar "pattern" most of my relationships had, and realized that I was the common denominator. It really wasn't about my ex-husband or the other men I had dated, it was about *me*. I was the one who had "done me wrong." Yikes! It was a shocking wake-up call and took me awhile to really grasp that I was the one who had made those choices. But, through the new personal and spiritual understandings I had, I grew, I forgave myself, and I learned.

I discovered some of the most important healing tools and skills of my life. I learned how to set intentions, vision for my future, release judgments of myself and others through self-forgiveness, expand my sense of self –worth, self-respect, self-acceptance, and self -love. I learned to clarify my needs and requirements for relationships. I developed a level of confidence I hadn't experienced before.

I also discovered how to take personal ownership of the relationships that had come my way, along with the experiences I had in them, how to let go, and learn from them. Most importantly, I came to the spiritual understanding that there is no separation between "me" and Spirit/God/Source, and with all of that awareness, along with the action steps I took using these new tools and skills, much of my world began to change.

And then I met my future husband. Was there a step-by-step process or system that I went through to finally meet the great love of my life? Was it an inner shift I had made? Was it luck, or was it just Divine timing that had my beloved show up? My conclusion was that it was a combination of the shift in my consciousness, the new skills I learned, the releasing I did of the past, the intention and vision I had for my future relationship, and the invisible power of Spirit at work on my behalf.

I felt so alive in this new marriage, and so full of love and inspiration, that I decided to translate it into a career and become a Relationship Coach, and combine it with the Intuitive Readings Business I already had. It has become a series of multiple blessings!

Today, as I write this I've been a happily married woman to the most amazing man for over 12 years. He's even more than I'd hoped for, visioned for, and dreamed of. He is the most kind, compassionate, loving, and affectionate man I've ever met. I'm showered with beautiful cards, words of love and affirmation, loving care, and lots of yummy backrubs. We are very much aligned in our core values, spiritual philosophies, relationship requirements, needs, shared interests, and compatibility. Plus, he even cooks for me!

I met him through the graduate school program that I had waited nine years to take, and must say that getting an M.A. and an M-r-s. were well worth the price of tuition! So, as I reflect on my history, I look back knowing that my journey – from feeling like a victim to feeling truly loved – unfolded exactly how it needed to, for me to learn what I needed in order to have the marriage I now have.

I have even made peace with those past experiences, knowing that the challenges and pain were stepping -stones for healing, learning, evolving, and ultimately manifesting.

Helping others prepare for, find, and live with the great love of their lives through my business has been an incredibly fulfilling experience. Guiding others through their journey to great love has touched my heart in so many ways. I love seeing the light shine in the eyes of others and feel the opening of their hearts as they meet, marry, or save their relationship with their beloved.

So, I share with all of you who are reading this, five things you can do to find love in your life:

Set a clear intention with a clear vision of what you want.

Become aware of triggers and wounds of your past so you can clear and heal them.

Connect with a higher power, whether you label it God, Source, Spirit, or the Universe, trusting that all has unfolded for your highest good.

Take ownership for how your life has unfolded, knowing you have free will and choices.

Live life with an open heart and an understanding that you are worthy of love and lovable.

My husband, who is a Chaplain for Hospice and counsels dying people and their families, says that as people are facing their last breath of their human experience, they're not concerned about career achievements they accomplished, cars they drove, homes they lived in, vacations they took. They care about *love*. Love they experienced with a partner or spouse, love they experienced with their families and friends. They can then transition in peace realizing how much they were loved. In the end, it's all about the love.

Susan's Take-Away "The most important lessons I learned in my search for the great love of my life was that I had to love and value myself first. It may sound cliché, but setting higher standards, being authentic, and letting go of the temptation to settle for anyone not aligned with who I was looking for, landed me as one of the two main characters in the greatest love story I've ever known."

The Magic of Crows

by Anna Huckabee Tull

"I have always been delighted at the prospect of a new day, a fresh try, one more start, with perhaps a bit of magic waiting somewhere behind the morning."
--J. B. Priestley

In my thirtieth year, the complex grown-up life I had carefully constructed suddenly came tumbling down all around me. My husband's interests had shifted to another woman, one who was an employee in the store that he and I ran together. Suddenly the business we had recently re-located to build up as a team felt like it could only hold one of us. And Dallas, the town we had relocated to from our cushy but stress-filled corporate lives in Chicago, housed many members of my husband's extended family but none of my own.

It had been a bold adventure: cashing in everything we had built up in our high-powered lives, purchasing a business together, and diving in, all in an attempt to revitalize our increasingly troubled relationship. And it had not played out well. One day we were scrambling to pull it all off, and the next, somehow, I found myself sitting in the rubble of those efforts. It began dawning on me that there was no longer any real place for me in this town, in this business, in this marriage.

As I sat there, startled and overwhelmed in the settling dust, I knew only that it was time to be moving away from this place. Where, I was not sure. I had not been tending the connections to my own family during the wild, grasping years of my invented-and-re-invented marriage.

But somehow I got into my car, pointed it toward Ohio, where I had grown up and where my parents still resided, and drove across the wide stretch of the US that separated me from there. When I got there, I found loving arms for lots and lots of sniffles and sobs.

And, too, I found that a close friend from high school had just gone through a divorce herself. A vacation was upon her. Since both of us were somewhat shell-shocked and overwhelmed with all the choices involved in building a new life from the ground up, we decided to escape together to Georgia for a few days of R&R.

The drive down was an unexpectedly light-hearted one, given our circumstances. We each found ways to cajole one another and take our minds off the heaviness of our current situations while easily reminiscing about earlier, simpler times.

As we drove, though, taking turns at the wheel, I began to notice something decidedly odd out the car windows. There seemed to be an unusual number of black birds. Were they crows? They were flying about, above us and along the side of the road. Not only that, but everywhere I turned, I seemed to be bumping into yet another representation of a crow. Sheila turned on the radio, and there was the band "Counting Crows" belting out a tune.

We stopped in a small town for lunch to find the only restaurant was "The Crow's Nest." The cashier at the gas station had a crow tattooed onto her arm. It went on and on like this, hours and hours on end, as we drove down towards the coast. I began asking everyone we met along the way, "What do you think crows stand for? What might it mean that I find myself seeing them, everywhere?"

At first oblivious to them unless I pointed them out, Sheila eventually began noticing them too. "There's another one of your crows," she would say. No matter how many of them I pointed out, they remained "my crows" in her mind, and, I suppose, in mine too. Somehow, although I knew this was unlikely and illogical, they all seemed to be appearing just for me.

The mystery and my search for an answer to it made for unusually intimate conversations with people I certainly never would have met otherwise. But nothing anyone offered up resonated deeply with me.

We completed our trip. We returned from our respite newly convinced that our divorces were survivable moments in our lives. But I had no more of a sense of direction than that it would be a good idea to return to my parents' house and let them feed and house me again. And as for my crow mystery, it remained unsolved, dangling up above me like a limp black clothesline sock in a slow wind.

Finally one evening, at my parents' house, still officially homeless, and probably stretching the limits of my parents' hospitality, I found myself outside in their backyard, steeping and stewing in their hot tub, on a cold April evening at dusk. As I sat there, a large black crow landed, literally, right on the edge of the tub. I felt as if it was looking directly *at* me, in to me, almost. It was black, and startling, moving its head in a jerky fashion. It opened its mouth and began to caw, almost felt as if it was chiding me.

"Come-ON! Come-ON! Come-*ON!*" it seemed to say. And in that flustered, strange moment, it hit me. An odd, somewhat antiquated phrase floated up into my consciousness. *As the crow flies.* The crow lifted itself by its great black wings and flew away. And as I sat there in the stillness of the aftermath, I began to understand.

As the crow flies. It's a phrase people sometimes use, when giving directions. "You go half a mile north, take a left at Miller's farm, go down that road for a mile, take another left and you're there. But as the crow flies, it's only about a mile." The most direct route, the one you would take if you could fly. "As the crow flies."

I felt something with me lifting up to a heightened perspective, rising up and up, above the full stretch of my entire life, as it had been lived, up until that very moment. There I was in my childhood years, following the flow. There I was in college, navigating new directions. Flying higher still, I could see it all: corporate opportunities, working my way up the ladder, the choice to marry, to relocate, chasing after each new solution to whatever problem was presenting itself to me at the moment. From up there I could see that there was no real pattern to it. Almost all of the choices of consequence in my life had been made looking only at what had been right in front of me: what was available, what seemed pressing, what was easy, what would allow for whatever was immediately concerning or uncomfortable to fade back out of range.

In a flash, in the long light of that chilled Midwestern evening, I saw that I had been navigating my life, my entire, precious life, based on reacting to whatever it was that was in front of me. In this moment, in the aftermath of the crow's visit, I began to know something new about myself. I began to feel, on an almost physical level, that a life looks very different from up above. I began to wonder what the shape of my life might be, moving forward from here, if I took a moment, just a simple moment, every now and again, to float above the path I was walking, and to consciously notice where it was that I was headed. And to then check that direction against my heart.

Imagine, I thought to myself, a life that looks far less haphazard than the path I have walked to this place. Imagine a life navigated and shaped *as the crow flies*: one where I take a moment to stand apart from the choices I have been making, where I look to see where things are headed, and begin to learn to make conscious choices about where I most want to steer, next. Imagine a life where I have chosen the direction I want to walk, not in reaction to what is in front of me, but in response to my very own heart and its whisperings.

Something shifted inside of me that evening. That very day, I began learning to float above my own life, periodically, and to lovingly adjust my course. I began asking important questions: Where do I *want* to be headed? Am I headed there? Which choices bring me more directly in line with my heart's deepest and truest desires? How do I invite in more of those kinds of choices?

Today I don't have to imagine any of these things. Today, years later, as I choose to skillfully, easily, regularly float above this life that I continue to create each day, I see a clear line: before and after the lesson of the crows. My path became clearer, smoother. It has arched forward into a beautiful loving relationship, a family, home, community, and a livelihood that makes my heart sing every single day. The new path of my navigation is as smooth and as artful as the one I have paved within myself, to my own heart and its deepest dreams and desires. From up above where I view it now, I honor the life I see below me with gratitude and deep joy: a life built consciously, with a heart wide open. It has been a long journey, but it's a clear, straight line, as the crow flies.

Anna's Take-Away "In living out this story, I learned how profoundly valuable it can be to navigate a life not from "down on the ground," making one decision at a time, based on what that moment holds in terms of hopes and fears, but from the vantage point of viewing it from far above. When we stop and step outside of the dramas we are living, we are filled with a powerful ability to navigate, joyfully, for our own highest good."

Healing with Ease, Grace and Laughter

by Thury Byrkett

"The practice of forgiveness is our most important contribution to the healing of the world."
--Marianne Williamson

Once my diagnosis, breast cancer, was confirmed my body felt as though it was spiraling down a drain. I felt a heaviness, spinning me and pulling me down. From that moment until the morning of my surgery, six weeks later, I felt as though fireflies were constantly buzzing inside of me. I thought this is crazy! Where was my *"self control, mind over matter, I can choose to feel ok"* attitude that I'd been living for the past 40 years? In my head I was saying, "Hold it together you're going to be fine", but my body was responding in its own way entirely! As it was happening I was fascinated yet utterly surprised at the disconnect between my head and the rest of my body.

I never asked "Why me?" My first thought was, "Ok, I guess this is going to be our next lesson in life." I kept seeing that side of me, the *knowing* side that I had seen reflected in the mirror at the imaging center. Logically, I accepted and understood that I was going to be going through this process, still totally unaware of exactly what it would end up being.

But still my body was in a constant state of hyper-static electricity. I knew this was going on, on behalf of my challenge – to use the skills and knowledge that I'd acquired over the years to find that peace within, and get my body into alignment with my thoughts.

I was constantly reminding myself that the universe had always provided exactly what I needed and that she would continue to do so this time too.

I kept thinking that if I have to go through this, then why not approach it and accept it with a loving, positive mind set. I had this overwhelming feeling that the choice was up to me. I could live in fear, or trust that everything was happening exactly as it should. I could live in fear or look for the lessons in all of this. I made my choice, ease and grace.

I began writing affirmations, set the intention to only use loving words when speaking of my experience, and I meditated every day. These were things that I'd been doing for years and had experienced the power of such commitments. I knew that in keeping with my familiar practices, I would find and maintain the peace that I would need to support me.

I began by letting go of some beliefs that I knew would never serve me throughout this experience. All my life I'd proudly taken care of myself with very little help from others. I knew that this was not going to be one of those times to try to do it alone. I let go of any negativity surrounding my thoughts about receiving help from others and allowing others to see my vulnerable side. I decided that this would be the best way to show myself the utmost level of self-love. Accepting my vulnerability ...not seeing this as a weakness but as a human emotion, part of my being that is neither positive nor negative. In accepting this aspect of myself, I opened up a channel that allowed more love, support and blessings than I ever could have imagined coming forward in my life.

Another area that needed healing surrounded my thoughts on self-worth. Letting go of the tape that would pop into my consciousness, telling me that I didn't have it as hard as others did so why should I feel special, or deserve to actually be able to experience this with ease and grace? The limiting belief that I had to release was that I was not powerful enough to do this on my own terms. There were times when I found myself wondering if I could actually "pull this off" and questioning whether or not my spiritual practice was strong enough to manifest something so big. As I thought about the issues of self worth and trust I kept being drawn back to thoughts of my birth. I was a preemie baby weighing only 2.9 lbs. when I was born. I stayed in the hospital for two months before I was stable enough for my parents to bring me home. I had never really thought about "why me?" or "how did I survive?" until this experience with cancer began. The night before my surgery I had such an incredible realization. Up until that point I had always thought of myself as extremely lucky to have survived being so small at birth and that I surely must have had guardian angels surrounding me. The truth is, I still believe in angels but something else became so clear to me that night. I realized that I had been strong enough to survive the odds then, and that I would be strong enough to survive the odds now. I suddenly came to the understanding that I *chose* to survive. *I chose* to live. *I chose* to be here. As an infant I had all the insight, self-love and self-worth that I needed to pull me through! How could I stop believing now? The answer: I couldn't and didn't! This was, by far, one of the most valuable lessons to come from this entire journey, and I carry the strength, courage and peace that followed that realization with me daily.

When I woke up in my hospital room following my bilateral mastectomy, the very first thought that came to me was..."This is it? I can TOTALLY do this!" When I was out of the hospital bed, sitting in front of the window a mere 24 hours after surgery, again I thought, "I can TOTALLY do this!" I don't want to imply that every single second of every single day was/is easy. Some days it takes a bit more effort, but I already know that I can do this and continue to do this on my terms. This is just the beginning of a lifetime of commitment to loving myself enough, trusting myself enough and believing in myself enough to stand firm in my truth, live every day in gratitude and continue to heal with ease and grace.

Even to this day, as I sit here typing, I am still amazed, grateful, astounded at how everything has unfolded and continues to unfold. I'm amazed at my body's strength and ability to heal. I'm grateful to my loving family, beautiful friends and incredible doctors. Lastly, I am astounded at how much I have learned about myself throughout this process. At times it feels as though this has been more about self-realization than cancer.

Since being diagnosed, I've had to make a lot of difficult decisions, which have required every ounce of faith and trust that I possess. And in those moments, or on those days when I feel challenged to stay positive, when the fear is testing my faith, I always return to how I felt waking up in that hospital room, and I know that I am totally doing this my way, with ease and grace. This is the first affirmation that I wrote after receiving my diagnosis.

I am a divine being, healing with ease and grace.

I am a radiant being and a beautiful example of perfect health.

I AM all of this and more!

Thury's Take-Away "From this experience I have learned the value of self-love and -trust. I have witnessed the power of positive thinking, perseverance, and faith and today, as I continue on my journey, I am LIVING with ease and grace."

Baby Hell, Baby Bliss

by Nancy Burcham

"Women need real moments of solitude and self-reflection to balance out how much of ourselves we give away." --Barbara De Angelis

I woke for the fifth time that night, roused out of a deep, weary sleep by the sound of my eight-month-old baby, Taylor, screaming in pain in the bed next to me. I never got used to it, this tiny human alarm with the lung power of an opera singer, jolting my body from slumber into a state of panic within seconds. As the adrenalin coursed through my veins and roused me thoroughly, the usual bag of mixed emotions flowed into my awareness: concern, love, fear, overwhelm, blame, guilt, frustration. My shoulder muscles already burned from the last four sessions trying to calm and comfort him, walking around the chilly garage for over an hour each time, in an attempt to let my husband, Max, sleep.

How could this be real? Eight months straight, of walking with him four or five times per night, while Taylor screamed at the top of his lungs for an hour or more each time, before he would fall asleep again for another hour, if I was lucky. Why couldn't anyone figure out what was wrong with him, or why he was in such obvious pain?

The daytimes weren't much easier, with him either nursing, vomiting, or crying most of the time. He rarely napped unless he was in my arms, on my breast, or in the car. Neither way was conducive to *me* getting any rest. I needed him to get better, so I could recuperate, too. I was exhausted and nearing the edge of my sanity.

The lows seemed insurmountable, at times. My body was crumbling apart at age 27: I'd suffered through the first six months of breastfeeding through multiple breast infections; hormones thrown off from the sleep deprivation and repeated adrenalin surges; upper back in constant pain; low back on the verge of going into spasm at any moment; head throbbing with migraines caused from lack of sleep. It was hard to find a moment to shower or care for myself in the most basic of ways. No one really understood what I was going through, except my husband and both sets of our parents, who had come out to help at times and had witnessed the unnerving reality of those nighttime crying sessions. Too many people offered unhelpful advice, encouraging me to "just let him cry," to put him in daycare, to give him formula, etc, etc. Depression was a constant companion. I had no energy to even laugh. I questioned why I ever thought having a baby would be a good idea. I wondered whether I had done something to cause his body to be in such distress.

Mostly, I judged myself for being so... human, for not remaining in a state of loving contentment with my baby at all times, for blaming him, being angry at him. I felt selfish and calloused when I did have to let him cry in order to take a shower or finish an important phone call...and guilty about my desire to escape sometimes. No matter how committed I was, or how much I sacrificed, I could find some way to criticize myself, for almost everything I did.

One particularly difficult afternoon, nothing was working to calm Taylor. I was frustrated and angry. Instead of my normal soothing tones, I found myself whispering "Shut up. Shut up. Shut up" as I walked with him around the room. He finally fell asleep on my shoulder from exhaustion, then startled awake as I tried to lay him down.

I snatched him up again harshly, cringing at my behavior, but unable to stop myself. I had seen other mothers do things like that to their babies or kids, and always felt so shocked and concerned. And now, here I was.

As Taylor screamed in my ear, my anger increased. I began yelling at him, as if he could understand. "What the hell do you want from me, little boy? I can't stand it any longer! I need you to just stop crying! Shut up and go to sleep! Leave me alone! Let me rest. Don't you see you are driving me crazy! I'm a worthless mother when you do this to me. What is wrong with you?"

On and on I ranted while he writhed and wriggled in my arms. He felt my stress and anger, which didn't help. Finally I held him out in front of me and looked him straight in the eye. "I guess you are just going to have to cry. I'm DONE with you!" I shouted, as I placed him firmly on the floor, walked out, and slammed the door. The shrillness of his scream only escalated through the closed door, but now it included his specific cry for me. "MAMA!! MAMA!!!" I could hear him crawling toward the door, his breath ragged and labored. I knew with that one word, he was saying what he couldn't say: "Don't leave me here alone! I need you, Mommy. You're my world! Why are you so mad at me? It's not my fault."

That made my guilt worse, but my anger worse as well. I couldn't stand that he wanted and needed me. And it pissed me off that he could be crying in pain for so long – struggling *against* me in my arms – and then shift instantaneously to this desperate plea for me to return. I turned away from the door, ran down the hall and flopped in front of the couch, punching it with a vengeance over and over, shouting "NO! NO! NO!"

I poured out all my anger at Taylor and at God for giving me this incredibly challenging baby to deal with. I hammered on that couch pillow for a few minutes straight. It scared me that I had that much anger inside, mostly aimed at my child. Taylor continued screaming for me from behind the door, which fueled my energy.

The phone rang. I picked it up and said hello, but didn't answer when Max asked how I was doing. I just walked over to Taylor's door, opened it, and shoved the receiver at Taylor's face, letting him howl into Max's ear like he had been howling into mine.

"Honey, are you ok?" (No response.) "Nancy, talk to me!" Max demanded. I still said nothing, just stared at the phone. Something about Max being on the other end of the phone, yet unable to give me any real help, was pushing me over the edge.

"Nancy. NANCY. Talk to me. What is going on?"

I shouted over Taylor's shrill wail, "What's going on is... I'm about ready to throw this baby out the window!" I finally broke down into an angry cry.

"Oh my God, honey. I'm coming home immediately!"

What kind of mother am I, that even my husband is worried about protecting our baby from me? I thought.

It had taken tremendous energy to keep myself from physically abusing Taylor, and to deny just how close I was to doing it on a regular basis. Because the truth was, today was an exceptionally bad day, but all that anger I launched at the couch pillows had been building over time. Yet, something about admitting my true feelings to Max broke the spell of denial I had been in.

I looked at Taylor's contorted face, screaming into the phone. He was now grabbing at my legs, pulling himself up and pawing at me to pick him up. His face was red and streaked with tears and sweat.

His mouth had been open wide for so long, it looked tight and rigid, like it had cramped in that position. His incredibly blue eyes were crystals of desperation looking up at me, fractured by the pools of water running over them.

I finally saw Taylor once again for what he was: a tiny child, dependent on me, entrusted to me, and in both physical and emotional pain. Probably more traumatized and confused than I was. In all his messiness, I saw his preciousness. My heart broke open with incredible sorrow and compassion for what he was experiencing in his small body.

I took a deep breath, and told Max, "No, it's ok. I'm not really going to do it. I was just that frustrated in that moment. You stay at work. I can get through this, like I've done before." When I turned to pick up Taylor, who was so exhausted himself, I cradled his head and body gently, whispered sweet, soothing sounds, and sat down in the recliner to nurse him once again. I had no idea how I would go on for months on end like this. But now that I'd diffused all the anger, and the denial had drained out of me, I found a new well of strength inside coming from a place of calm.

As Taylor latched on and his ragged crying stopped, I gazed at his perfect profile, and then became completely flooded with awe as I thought about the miracles of my creation:

that my body somehow knew how to create this little being out of two microscopic cells;

that specific genes had converged to give him my lips, ears and eyebrows;

the wonderment of how my breasts could produce the type and volume of milk to sustain him completely; the new empowerment I felt in my body. After struggling with body image my entire life, I had experienced through pregnancy that my body was doing something really GOOD; and, the incredible depth of love I felt for this Being and soul that had chosen me as his mother for some reason, had grown inside my body for nine months, and who was now so dependent upon me.

There was nothing else so gratifying, ever. I became unaware of anything but absolute bliss. No worry about how to get through the day or another month. No feelings of guilt or blame. Nothing but the love, and the miracle of this life I had created. Somehow, through Grace, the windows had been thrown wide open again, allowing me to see myself and Taylor in the divine circle of creation.

I realized all Beings, in our humanness, are all just doing the best we can at every given moment. Because if we *could* be doing any better, we *would* be. How can I ask any more of myself, or of anyone else?

Sometimes, when we are pushed to the edges of our physical and emotional strength, we are forced to find our reserves from a place we never knew existed. Without a doubt, the depth of love, strength and commitment I found for my son *because* of our trials was the greatest gift I received.

Nancy's Take-Away "The most important learning for me was to reveal my true feelings – they aren't bad, they just are. Then to express the anger, in a non-harming way, and just get that energy out of my body. That is the only way I had a chance to NOT do something abusive to my child, and to open myself to the incredible moment of grace, compassion and bliss."

Through My Kitchen Window

by Maryellen Bein

"Waking up this morning, I smile. Twenty-four brand new hours are before me. I vow to live fully in each moment." -Thích Nhất Hạnh

Through my kitchen window

the morning begins.

I scan the sky,

look for clues as to what is before me.

magnificence, beauty and glory

radiate in various shades as the horizon slowly,

ever so slowly, opens up and shows itself to me.

Through my kitchen window

miracles appear, nature guides my eyes

and touches my heart.

there is an awakening, a knowing unfolding,

filling me with peace that all is well...

colors take on a deeper vibrance as the sky lifts its veil

and warm beams of pink awaken the feathered creatures;

they chant their song...

to stir trees, move sap, uncurl leaves,

to awaken blossoms shining with the morning
diamond drops of dew.

Through my kitchen window

the stage of life produces simple wonder,

often showing me another facet of what it is

just now, in this precious moment of being.

Life is, I am... that is certain.

Through my kitchen window I am greeted,

as I greet the day,

opening my heart, being filled,

aligning with that which is

downloading an image, thought or feeling

gifted to me through framed glass.

My waking, walking morning meditation has begun

through my kitchen window

Maryellen's Take-Away "Living in the Heart of the Midwest in Indiana I have the privilege of experiencing Mother Nature and her Four Seasons. Each morning I connect to that vast omnipresence over the sink out through my kitchen window. There is always something to draw my attention, a gift, a thought for the day."

Waiting For Happiness

by Teresa McKee

"Happiness is not something ready-made. It comes from your own actions." --Dalai Lama

As a 13-year old, I lived in a dysfunctional, violent household, but I knew I was on this earth to do something important. I knew I'd be happy as soon as I earned a scholarship and became a famous lawyer, righting all of the wrongs in the world.

The situation at home only grew worse and I ran away from home at 16. Having my first child at 17, I realized the scholarship dream was over, but I was determined to be happy, so I changed my plan. I'd get married, have four children, and be the best stay-at-home mom ever. We'd live in a nice little house, maybe even with a white picket fence. Then I'd be happy.

I married at 18 and had my 2nd child at 19. We could barely make ends meet with both of us working, so I knew the big family with the white-picket fence wasn't happening. I altered my plan again. As soon as the kids were in school, I'd go to college and start a new career. By the time I was 20, I knew I wanted to be a writer.

As my youngest child hit four years old, I began to anticipate attending school. I loved my children dearly, and I wasn't miserable, but I knew I'd be truly happy once I started on my path as a writer.

That same year, my husband received news that we were being transferred across the country. This was exciting news, but I felt that familiar "here we go again" niggle in the back of my brain. Moving out of state would mean waiting a year to establish residency before I could attend college. So, I adjusted my happiness-plan one more time. I would get us settled into a new community and find a job to help us financially until I could start school. Then I would be really happy.

Little did I know at the time, but the out-of-state transfers became a regular part of his career. I had gone from Texas to New Mexico to New York to Wisconsin by the time I was 26 years old, with two children, no career, and a feeling that my turn was not going to come.

The children were thriving and we'd become very close due to being thrown into strange cities together and with my husband gone half the time traveling for work. In Wisconsin, I finally made the one-year mark and enrolled in a private women's college in Liberal Arts. I flourished and was so happy, at least while I was in school. I had to continue working and there was always so much to do between the kids' school activities, holding down the fort in my husband's absence, and getting my homework done between classes. I told myself just to ride through it, because on the other end of this exercise was true happiness.

Before I could attain my degree, my husband announced that we were being transferred again, to California. I set my jaw and convinced myself that I could do it. We hadn't been in California two years before the next transfer came up. I could not do it again.

The children were too old for it not to negatively impact them to leave school and their friends, and I could not keep postponing my life with constant moves. We made the decision that my husband would change careers. I would put him through school and when he was done, I would quit my job and write full-time. This time, it would be a four-year delay in attaining my happiness.

My husband started a program to become a sports therapist. He was excited and it was contagious. But three years into a program full of science and anatomy, sports therapy became impacted in California. This meant a much longer haul and a much diminished chance of getting a job when he graduated. We decided it was better for him to switch to his second career choice, teaching history, but this meant starting almost from scratch. I kept up a pretty good front, but inside, I felt my happiness flame flickering.

During his education, my job (which I never considered my career) flourished. I received promotions and raises at a steady pace and even bought a small home while he was in school. I was marking time though, waiting for my turn.

After several set-backs and nine years from the original start of his career change, my husband was in his last year of graduate school. He had clearly found his calling and was going to have a fantastic career. I was feeling a small spark of hope for the first time in several years. I'd been through a very challenging decade, but had stayed the course. My turn was finally coming.

I was very close to both of my daughters, now fully grown, and had two adorable grandchildren. I loved my son-in-law like my own child and we had a house full of people all of the time. And now I was at the threshold of my new career. True happiness, finally! My mentor, my grandmother, passed away in August of 2001, and while I was saddened and felt a profound loss, I was grateful that I'd flown out to see her a few weeks prior to her departure.

Upon my return, my oldest daughter moved back in with us, with her two children, vaguely explaining that she was unhappy. The more I pressed to find out why she would leave her husband, the more withdrawn she became. The Labor Day weekend before 9/11, she blew. She declared she was unhappy and could not possibly be "perfect" like me. She announced that she was leaving the family and told my grandchildren to tell me good-bye. She left her husband, her friends and all of her family. I never saw her again.

The utter shock of that night felt unbearable. It was completely unexpected and unexplainable. I went through days of all of her friends, aunts, uncles, grandparents, and coworkers that had known her since childhood, asking for answers, to which I had none. I became severely depressed. I was still in a deep state of shock when 9/11 occurred. As I watched those towers fall, I felt they symbolized my life. It, too, felt like it was imploding. As with the rest of the country, I was upset and nervous, wondering what was happening, both to my life and to my country. I stumbled through life, unable to get my bearings or comprehend what was happening.

And then just weeks later, I discovered that my husband was having an affair. I'd waited all of this time to be happy and now it was all being taken away from me. I filed for divorce without even discussing it with him. The triple-hit of my grandmother passing, my daughter and grandchildren vanishing from my life and my husband's betrayal were more than I could handle.

In a flash, I went from being the perfect wife, perfect mother and perfect employee, to being a shell of a human being, barely able to function. But just as I felt that life was over, that there was absolutely no point to living, a tiny spark in my heart started pushing me. In the beginning, with one foot in front of the other, I kept going. I realized that maybe the problem was me. Maybe I was living life all wrong.

I returned to studying spirituality, which I had done most of my life, but which had fallen to the wayside with my busy schedule during the past few years. As I reintroduced myself to the concept that we are not here on earth to suffer, I had an epiphany. I had been suffering and it was all self-inflicted. I had a misperception about how life was supposed to work.

I noticed from photographs that I had deep laugh lines at the corners of my eyes, with white stripes in the summer because I laughed so much, the sun didn't get a chance to color them. I had lived an interesting, joyful adult life for 25 years, but hadn't recognized it as happiness because I had created a rule, a box that equaled happiness in my mind, and my life hadn't fit that picture.

Instead of feeling resentment toward my daughter who had "left me," I gained acceptance that as a mother, all I wanted for my daughter was for her to be happy. I forgave myself for judging myself as a bad mother.

I raised a child who had the courage to do what she needed to, in order to be happy. My husband hadn't betrayed me. He was just searching for happiness in the wrong place, too. We're best of friends now. And there was never anything preventing me from becoming a writer but that silly rule in my head about what it had to look like.

It took me several years and a lot of inner work to learn that happiness does not come from the outside, but from within. Happiness is a choice! I have a beautiful life and am grateful every day for all of the experiences that have enriched it. I am now a mother, a grandmother, a friend, a mentor, a writer, a counselor, a student and a very happy person! But it was out of utter despair that I discovered my true identity, a loving soul, and now live a joyful, purpose-driven life.

Teresa's Take-Away "The lesson I took away from my story was that it affirmed my path and confirmed that when I let go of deciding how something should happen and just focus on what I want to happen, it happens! As I have continued to be open to the possibilities, the possibilities continue to unfold. I have more than enough joy, health and abundance than I would have ever thought possible before I discovered my way. You can, too!"

Are You Listening to Me?

by David Cooper

"Too often we underestimate the power of a touch, a smile, a kind word, a listening ear, an honest compliment, or the smallest act of caring, all of which have the potential to turn a life around."
--Leo Buscaglia

It's hard to listen to your boss when you don't just dislike him, but you hate him. Why couldn't I even look at him? Why had I taken this job? Why was everything so messed up? I could feel tears in my eyes, a pain in my stomach and a headache that was tight around my scalp. I felt like crying or screaming that I couldn't do it anymore. I couldn't be positive, or try hard, or be a good employee. I felt broken by this man, worthless and stupid. I wanted to walk out of his office, past all the rows of people working, past the security guard and out the door to never come back. I held onto the sides of the chair with both hands to stop myself from leaving his office. I gripped so tightly that my hands were hurting and my fingers were white.

"This is not a plan. I need a plan. OK?"

"OK."

"I don't think you get it because I have told you before. This is not a plan and I need a plan. OK?"

I mumbled, although I had no idea what he wanted. I thought I had given him a plan but the twenty pages I had worked on were in the garbage. They weren't right. I was a flop. I felt like I was a little boy who had just peed on the floor, even though he had tried to hold it until he got to the bathroom.

I was ashamed. I was desperate. I was ready to give up not just on this job, but also, even on life.

The next day, I complained about him to a woman I had never met before. A friend of a friend, Dana, was having a small gathering at her house. "Whatever I do is never good enough. I'm never going to please him. He's just a jerk. I feel stupid that I am so triggered by him. It's just a job but I am so miserable when I'm there. I can't stop thinking about work."

She didn't say anything but I knew that she was listening to me like no one had ever listened to me before. She sat waiting for me to speak. A listener not a talker, I thought. "I mean he's a smart guy. I just can't stand him. What do you think I should do?"

"The only way you can heal an issue like this is to pour love on the problem." I looked at her blankly. What was she talking about? How could I love someone whom I couldn't even bear to be in the same room with? I felt annoyed that I had trusted her with my problem. She obviously didn't have a clue. "Put him up on your screensaver at work." "Sit opposite him and look at him in meetings." "Love him!" She smiled.

A wave of peace washed over me. I suddenly felt calm for the first time in months. I couldn't understand why I felt so good. Then I realized. I knew in my heart that she was right. I had learned through my spiritual work that whatever I focused on was what I would get. If it were positive, I would get more positives. If it were negative, I would only receive more negatives.

My mind stopped racing and a warm glow radiated from inside me and made me stop and enjoy the purity of the moment. But even though I knew what I was supposed to do, I couldn't. I just couldn't.

I couldn't turn off that hate and replace it with love. It was impossible. I felt my body tighten up and the thoughts race around my head again.

The next week, I found myself back in his office. It was going to be another of those meetings when I would listen to what he said and pretend that I had understood what he wanted, even though I had no clue. Every muscle was tense. I felt afraid of what he was going to say and even more afraid of what he might say.

But he was smiling. He was making small talk. I began to panic. This was even worse. It was like the spoonful of sugar, which is supposed to make the medicine go down, but will never ever mask that bitter after-taste. I felt hysterical. I was screaming except nothing was coming out of my mouth. This was going to be the moment when I quit, or when he fired me. I was ready for that punch in the belly.

But then something he said made me pay attention. He was not talking about work but about his childhood. "I liked art. But my school – you know – nobody did – nobody – so I got picked on a lot. I got beaten up some. I was this skinny kid. It was bad – bad. I couldn't get home without getting kids jumping me."

I looked at him and instead of the man I loathed, I saw a boy, someone who didn't fit in and was getting punched and kicked, forced onto the floors by boys who were bigger and tougher than him. My school had been on the right side of the tracks and I had never been beaten up or bullied or cursed at. Yet this man had. I suddenly felt empathy for him. A feeling of love for this man I hated. How strange!

I realized that given when he had grown up, what he had put up with, and what he had learned, he was doing really well. He was a manager in a large company and he was doing the best he could. Really! I felt a wave of compassion for this small boy who was sitting in front of me dressed up like a big tough-guy-boss.

How could I hate someone like this? Of course he wasn't perfect, but who would be, given what he had gone through? And suddenly I realized I could love him.

As I let down the shield and sword I had been using against him, I experienced calm and quiet. I realized that I was experiencing a moment of happiness, but it was such an unfamiliar idea that my mind couldn't understand it.

So from that point on, I sat opposite my boss and made myself make eye contact. I found a picture of the department personnel with him front and center, and put it up on my notice board. I made myself think of him. I followed Dana's advice. And I felt more content, less stressed and more able to be strong in who I was. Most importantly, I put down my hatred for this man. I looked inside of me and explored what I was supposed to learn from my boss.

I already knew that he was not a bad person and that given all he had learned growing up, he was doing the best he could with the tools he had. I forgave him. I felt like shouting out with joy. I was smiling. I was OK. But there was more. What did this mean for me? What was my boss teaching me?

I sat in the quietness of my office in Los Angeles, looking out over the lemon tree and watching the humming birds go past, but instead I saw a cold damp backyard in London.

I was alone, playing with my Legos, making imaginary houses filled with imaginary furniture. My parents were inside. My mother was cooking a cake for our tea and my father was watching soccer on TV.

I felt connected to my mom but not to my dad. I so wanted to please him but even then, at the age of nine or ten, I had given up. I hated sports. He loved them. I loved antiques and art. He tolerated museums. I was confusedly gay. He was clearly straight. I wanted him to love me but I didn't know how. He didn't understand me and I didn't understand him. I was rejected and shunned by him, or so it seemed, a lonely and alone boy.

The tears were making tracks down my cheeks as I thought about my father. Sad for the kind of childhood I had fantasized about, but which had not happened. Deep sobs were coming up in my throat. I was so sad that my heart hurt.

I knew that my relationship with my boss was just like my relationship with my father. That lack of communication, fear of saying something wrong, and that aching desire to please him were exact in every detail. I wasn't good enough. I wasn't enough. And I was not what he wanted in son. I couldn't believe it because it wasn't true. These feelings for my dad were in the past. I had let them go when he died. At his memorial service back in England, I had been amazed at how many of his friends had come up to me and greeted me like a long-lost friend. I didn't know many of them but they all seemed to know me.

"Oh you're the one who lives in America. Your dad told us how you took him to New York and that Mall of America. He said he couldn't believe it."

"Yes and this is Ed. He mentioned your partner."
"You're a writer. That's what I heard."

For a man who didn't understand me and who didn't care about me, his friends certainly knew a lot about me. The only conclusion a sane person could come to, was that he cared about me and shared his pride in me with his buddies.

As each elderly man or woman approached me I felt more and more guilty at my lack of faith in my dad's love. I felt true loss as I realized what my father had been to me. And I drank in the caring, compassion and love his friends had for him and me.

I forgave my father, I forgave my boss, but most importantly I forgave myself for believing the stories I had created about myself and my relationships with my dad and my boss. I was loved and I was love, and that was the whole truth and nothing but the truth.

David's Take-Away "I learned that I was in charge of my life. I could decide what I wanted at work and I could make anything happen."

Leaving

by Linda Luke

"So many people prefer to live in drama because it's comfortable. It's like someone staying in a bad marriage or relationship - it's actually easier to stay because they know what to expect every day, versus leaving and not knowing what to expect."
--Ellen DeGeneres

I had been walking around bent over at the waist for days in a feeble attempt to protect myself. I could feel him watching me, looking for any opportunity to attack. "It won't hurt." he said. "One quick punch in the stomach and the baby will be gone." All I knew was I didn't want to get hit anymore.

He was a friend of my father's who I thought I could trust. Once he said he loved me, it was easy to convince me to go away with him because it felt like a miracle that I could be loved at all. It was there, 3000 miles away from my family and home. Then I learned about his alcoholism and drug use. I learned about fear, violence, abuse, and what it was like to feel hopeless. I was only 17.

I call those my zombie years. Something inside of me broke and I shut down. It was as if I stopped thinking and feeling and was just putting one foot in front of the other in order to survive. I was completely numb and the daily reminders of my unworthiness convinced me I was not capable of taking care of myself if I tried to leave. So, I stayed.

My pregnancy was a rough one. I was very ill and there was seldom food in the house. My son's father continued to spiral downward. He flaunted an affair with our neighbor and I continued to experience abuse. My son was born two months premature and we both spent a month in the hospital fighting for our lives. The first time I saw my sweet baby he was in an incubator with tubes connected to him everywhere. I was allowed to touch his hand through a protective sleeve, but he didn't move or respond. My heart was wide open with love and broken at the thought of what he was going through.

My son came home from the hospital when he reached five pounds and our new life began. His father tried to stay and do the right thing, but soon returned to his old patterns. His drinking kept me in a constant state of fear as I tried to stay safe until he would crash, usually throwing up, crying, and begging for my forgiveness.

That final night started like many others. He came home after drinking with friends, barely able to walk, and made a mess by throwing eggs around as he tried to make himself breakfast. I laid low and after a while it seemed like he was winding down and we would be safe, so I decided to go sleep with my baby in his room.

I was just dozing off when my son's father came crashing into the room, yelling and grabbing me. It took a moment to remember where I was and that my son was next to me. When I did, I went into a panic. My son was in danger! My baby could get hurt! And, that is when it clicked. It was suddenly very clear. This is not right. This is not okay. This is not what we deserve and I am no longer willing to live this way. I picked up my son and ran for safety. I felt solid, sure, and confident for the first time in a long while.

The next morning was filled with tearful apologies and promises, but I knew what I had to do. It wasn't long before I was sitting behind the wheel of our old car, my son next to me and our clothes in the back seat. I had nowhere to go. My parents even declined to take us in. I did not know what I was going to do. I just knew that we were leaving and, somehow, deep inside I knew we were going to be okay.

I won't pretend that life was easy after we left. I felt ashamed to have to ask for emergency assistance, but I did. We found a place to stay and a friend helped me get a job where she worked. Everything felt new and scary, but I was determined to create a better life for my son. Each step of the way I gained confidence and felt a little better about myself. I pushed myself to succeed at work and learned that being a single mother can be challenging, but we had a decent life and most of all, we were safe.

My experience with my son's father continued to play a role in how I felt about myself and what I believed about the world. For years I suffered silently with undiagnosed depression and frequent excruciating migraines. I still believed that all I deserved was a life of hardship and struggle. I felt a deep sense of unworthiness and had humiliating anxiety attacks that made me cry in public. And then, it all caught up with me. Pushing myself, the headaches, and the emotional pain of my past brought me to the brink of exhaustion. I remember feeling that my spirit would die if I didn't do something drastic.

So, I did. I dropped everything to attend a workshop I heard about. This was a huge step outside my comfort zone and triggered a whole new set of fears and anxieties.

I would be spending money on myself, getting on an airplane for the first time, and putting myself in a new situation where I had no control. As if that wasn't enough, I was committing to being vulnerable and open with a group of complete strangers. I was terrified.

By the time I got there I was an emotional mess. And then, a beautiful thing happened. The man teaching the workshop walked up to me, looked me in the eyes, and said, "I will be safe for you so that you can do the work you came to do." Something in me broke open. That one sentence freed me up to invest fully in the experience. I will be forever grateful because it is there that I started my journey of letting go of my past and made the decision to hire a Life Coach who could support me in moving forward.

The first call with my coach was a free consultation and I remember worrying she might tell me I was beyond hope and reject me. Instead, she started the call with her intention to be supportive and safe. She listened carefully to what I said and asked questions that woke up new ideas in my mind. The insights she gave were powerful, but it was that sweet, safe feeling that let me know she was the right coach for me and I committed to working with her on a weekly basis.

In the beginning I would get nervous about our calls thinking my coach would judge me harshly if I revealed my true self, but she was gentle and patient with me. She saw through the issues to the truth of who I was, and I learned I could tell her anything. My coach held a higher vision for me than I could have ever dreamed of for myself and I often wondered if she was an angel in disguise.

Healing my life was not necessarily a straight path. My journey included ups and downs, laughter and tears, and a whole lot of learning.

It felt like I was shedding the things that did not support me and bringing in things that would. I remembered that I am a soul in a human body and began to feel more peaceful, loving, and empowered. The biggest surprise of all was that I felt called to study life coaching and spiritual psychology so that I could share the gifts I received with others who wanted to change their lives.

My journey continues even today. That little baby I fought so hard for is now a loving father who has given me three grandchildren that I adore. I can truly say that my life has shifted from fear, pain, and hopelessness to one that is truly blessed. I love my work as a coach, blogger, and facilitator and how it allows me to support others as I share my message of hope, possibilities.

Linda's Take-Away "The first step in creating a life I love was realizing that I deserved more than being abused. Making that one internal shift allowed me to start believing in other possibilities for my son and me. It gave me the courage to leave and accomplish things I would never have dreamed were possible."

The Essence of Life

by Laurel Airica

"To be yourself in a world that is constantly trying to make you something else is the greatest accomplishment." --Ralph Waldo Emerson

"What is the Essence of Life," I asked.

I need to find out fairly fast
and I'd like it to be in rhyming verse:
profound, definitive – yet terse.
"The Essence of Life," the Angels said,

*"is to live while you're living – **and** after you're dead.
For there's never a time when you'll cease to exist;
so, it's best to say YES and not try to resist."*

I know perfectly well life is not evanescent.
But you've given its purpose.
I asked for Life's essence.

So, I walked to the Ocean to speak with the Sea.
We communicate with High Frequency.

I posed the question
and here's what She gave:

*"The Essence of Life is a friendly wave.
Like sea and sand, it's waves and particles ..."*

Just as I'd read in those technical articles.
But hardly the basis for eloquent poetry.

So, I was relieved to recall that I know a Tree
who gives me leafs for my writing abundantly.
Surely, She'd answer me more fundamentally.

She nodded and boughed,
whispered that she'd be proud
to assist me in knowing my reason for Being.

But said,

"You're not a bit metaphysically fit
for the answers are everywhere.
You're just not seeing:

The purpose of Life
is the same as its essence –
WHATEVER you do, try to be in the Presence.
For the prize isn't won by the joyless and dutiful.
And Life won't become fun till you choose to

BE-YOU-TO-FULL!"

Laurel's Take-Away The story recounted in this
poem is true, both literally and metaphorically. I had
no idea how completely true it was until I reflected on
the messages. I hope it encourages you as it did me
to always do your best to be yourself to the fullest!

The Power of a Prayer

by Dayna Dunbar

"Prayer is not an old woman's idle amusement. Properly understood and applied, it is the most potent instrument of action." --Mahatma Gandhi

I had to think long and hard to draw from my memories a single incident with my Grandma Weezie, when I was asked by my family to write about one for her 90th birthday celebration. As I scan my life with Grandma, it seems like pretty much every memory has the taste and smell of food – Christmas pie, Thanksgiving turkey, Easter ham, dollar pancakes on a Sunday morning, fried chicken on a regular but still holy day (any day that included Grandma's fried chicken was holy), Halloween candy and church cookies. Most all of the memories also include Grandma somehow making me feel special – presents under the tree, the sweetest witch the world has ever seen dressed up just for us kids, a magical trip to Frontier City or a huge banana split. In that memory, she warned me, but I ate it all anyway and threw up on the linoleum floor of Snyder's Grocery Store. Oh yes, that reminds me, I loved grocery shopping with Grandma. Come to think of it, I loved doing anything with her, except maybe getting my allergy shots, but even that turned out OK because I had Grandma and my mom all to myself. Afterward, they'd take me to McDonald's, which was a very big deal for us back then. See? With Grandma, it always comes back to food.

But, miraculously, my favorite memory doesn't include food at all. It was a gorgeous but windy spring day about six or so years ago when my partner Brenda and I went back to my small hometown in Oklahoma for a visit. I wanted to film Grandma Weezie and Grandpa Alvie in their original habitats – out at the farms they grew up on. The two of them, Brenda and I piled into Grandma's car and went out to Grandpa's homestead, where Grandma first moved in when she married him at all of sixteen years old. They told us stories, and as always, it sounded like a hell of a lot of work – pioneer work, manual labor, carving a living out of the land with a tractor and your bare hands, feeding a whole gob (as my mama says) of family and farmhands with a stove and a work ethic the size of the oak tree out in the front yard.

After talking about all that work, Grandpa had to take a nap, so we dropped him off and drove out to West Point Farm where Grandma was born and raised. It was back past the hard labor to a time for Grandma of innocence and joy. I love when she talks about growing up with her folks. How her daddy said, as the youngest, she was made from scraps, being so tiny when all the rest of them were big boned and tall. I love that she was doted on by her parents and her big brothers and sisters, how she felt so loved, so complete, so part of something good and honest and true. She told me that day how, if it was discovered that a man was hitting his wife, all the men would get together and go to his house and put a stop to it. "There was no police back then. The men took care of these things." I love that too. And the irony of it when she says, "If Dad knew there was a woman preacher at the First Christian Church, he'd roll over in his grave."

After looking at the farm, the land where this woman of compassion and dignity grew up, we got the key from Charlotte Novak and went to West Point Church. How do I describe the moment of entering that place? I guess the grandest cathedral couldn't have been any more filled with the presence of Christ's love. And how do I know what that feels like? Because I learned it through my grandmother. The sun slanted in through the windows of the sanctuary, and the air was still like heaven.

Our voices sounded magnified in that stillness, so we naturally talked softer. And that was perfect, because it was a time for soft words. Grandma told Brenda and me the history of the church, how her dad had helped to build it, how they went every Sunday and all their community and social events centered around it. We went to the front and sat in the first pew, and because one of my favorite things in the world is to hear Grandma pray, I sure wasn't going to miss the chance hearing her devotion in this place. And this is when the light on the whole day turned up even more, like the sun shining brighter than it already was in a clear blue sky.

Grandma said a prayer for me and Brenda, for us together, for our lives, our happiness and our safety. She could have prayed about anything. I guess I expected her to ask for God to look out for her family, for continued blessings on West Point Church or for grace for her relatives who had passed, for healing of illness or peace or anything. But she prayed for me and my partner, a prayer so sweet and simple and pure that it still rings like a high church bell in my heart.

Now, a lot of people might take this for granted. But it was something I never thought I'd experience in my life. Not tolerance of the fact that I am gay, or mere acceptance, but a blessing, a blessing on our family's holy ground. It was from her, from Weezie, from the person I most want to be blessed by in the world.

And, of course, the prayer has worked. Brenda and I are happier than ever, coming up on ten years in a few months. We still talk about that prayer. In fact, it was Brenda who reminded me of it again just recently when Grandma nearly flew into a tizzy when she realized she hadn't written Brenda's Christmas check yet (she could no longer shop). I think it was December 20th. I told her she had plenty of time, but she took out her checkbook and pen right then and nearly threw it at me. I thought we were going to have to get out the Xanax. Tears came to my eyes. When I told Brenda about this incident, she said, "I love your grandma. She's always been so good to me. Remember that prayer she said for us?" Oh, yes, we both will always remember that prayer.

Dayna's Take-Away "Through this experience and many others in her life, my grandma taught me how to keep my heart open even when my ideas of right and wrong are challenged. It also taught me not to limit what miracles and wonders can happen in this life. This was a moment I never, ever thought would happen and yet, it did and in such a beautiful moment of unfolding."

Leap of Faith

by Jeanne Michele, PhD

"There are many talented people who *haven't fulfilled their dreams because they over-thought* it, or they were too cautious, and were unwilling to make the leap of faith." --James Cameron

Leap of Faith: *An abrupt or precipitous passage, shift, or transition; Belief that does not rest on logical proof or material evidence.*

Leaping into the void of the unknown is like free falling from outer space to earth. You are never quite sure exactly where and how you will land. Survival is often questionable. My 15 ½ year-old son and I held hands and leapt together when we packed up our lives to embark upon a 2,000 mile cross-country journey, leaving behind the only home we had ever known to begin a new life together. (The italicized text in the story which follows has been taken from my journal writings at the time of the move.)

"I have done it! I have really done it. I have left home. I left it all behind. The reality of it all is sometimes very scary and sometimes incredibly exciting. I just can't believe it. I sold our house. I miss it already. The home we built is now just a memory. It belongs to someone else now. That may have been the most difficult of all, leaving it behind. I loved the backyard, the view, the Christmas tree we planted, now brown and withered. It died and we never really gave it a proper burial. Now it just stands there brown and lifeless. Just like us, it couldn't quite survive the climate. Maybe that was a sign. Nothing grows here. Even still, it was hard to leave."

"Different is not necessarily better." I recall those words of a friend just before we left. I suppose that is true, although those aren't the farewell words explorers hope to hear prior to embarking upon the discovery of a new land! My friends tried to be supportive, but their view of California was shaped by the tabloids, unpredictable and shaky. They didn't understand the ache in my soul beckoning me home, to my new home.

I had such an optimistic spirit, like I had when my ex-husband and I first met. I fell for the cool guy with the black Mustang convertible who lived two doors down from me. Seventeen years old and he had his own car. I was lucky if I occasionally got to drive my mom's car to the grocery store alone. Cool car. Cool guy. I fell hard. Even though there were a million reasons to leave during the course of my eighteen-year marriage, time and time again I chose to stay. Perhaps leaving my home town was the only way I could really let this man go and truly discover myself. I realize that I had lost me somewhere along the way and was determined to get her back, to discover her anew.

"Old dreams shattered. New dreams waiting to be born. Am I brave or incredibly foolish to move so far away to do something I am feeling called to do even though I don't really know what it is. I just know I need to go. Brave, I think. Maybe. At least I hope so. A life veiled in chaos is not free. How nice it will be to leave the chaos behind and create a peaceful life. This is my hope at least. I believe I can. And yet sometimes I wonder if chaos has become comfortable, like the worn blanket you just can't seem to give up."

Looking back on the angst I personally experienced, leaving my husband and home behind, helps me to better understand how difficult walking away can be. Even when you know it's the best choice. It felt like I was ripping out a piece of my heart and leaving it behind. Till death do us part. Even though physically alive, part of me died a long time ago. I loved the man, but it was clear I could no longer live with him. Life was giving me and my son a ticket out and I knew we had to take it.

"There is more for me for sure. I just know there is more. I want to teach my son there is a better way to do life. This is our time to heal. To grow. To create a better life. God help us. I want more for my son than he has had. He is a good kid. He has a kind heart. He deserves more. I want him to recover the lost pieces of life that were stolen from him. Living with the instability of alcohol, which can rear its frightening head at any moment, is no way to raise a child. Peaceful moments are fleeting. Sure there are fun times, but you never quite know when the crazy will kick in, and we certainly had plenty of crazy."

I was leaving life-as-I-knew-it behind to embark upon my own personal "California Dreamin'" story. I had been offered a new job where I knew no one outside of the few people who worked for the branch of the company inviting me out.

I prayed a lot. Searching for signs to guide my choice, I flew to California to check it out. I spent a weekend there, walking on the beach and talking to anyone who would listen. When asked how they liked living here people answered in one of two ways. Either they loved it and never wanted to leave, or hated it and were looking to move as soon as possible. There wasn't much in between. I lit candles. I called in the angels. I paid attention to all the signs. I was on my own *Celestine Prophecy* quest.

Ultimately I got my answer. This was an important leap to make. I made one more journey westward with my son. We called in the angels. We discussed the move. He was in. We were like two voyagers saying a few Hail Marys and crossing our fingers for good measure before leaping into the unknown together. Unbeknownst to us both, at the time, the inner journey upon which we were about to embark was probably far more challenging than the outer one.

I was beginning my job. Not just any job, but my dream job. I would be heading up an entirely new training department for a highly successful region of the company. Training was something I always wanted to do. I was the first one in the company to play this role. My excitement quickly overshadowed the fear, at least for the most part. I was thrilled with the new opportunity.

From the beginning it was clear to me that there was another reason why I was supposed to leave. There was something important outside of the company that I was also being called to do, or experience. I didn't know what it was at the time, but I trusted the wisdom of my heart, which was calling me forward. I had faith that life would reveal its plan to me when it was time. I now realize this was the deep driving force behind the decision to move.

Had I known then that later that summer my son would go back home to visit his dad and decide that he wanted to move back to the Midwest, I probably never would have made the move. Not in a million years would I have chosen to create a life without my son. And yet, in the fall of that year I had sold my home, become well-entrenched in a new career, and my son was not with me. The sadness was almost unbearable.

Nothing I could do or say would make him change his mind. He missed his friends. He missed his hometown. I pleaded with him on the phone to come back, but his mind was made up. He was not coming back to live. I would have to settle for periodic visits during school breaks.

His dad was no help either. He missed his son and I am sure encouraged him to stay. I now had to face the fact that my son was going back into a toxic world where he would have to figure out life on his own. He had returned to the environment we fought so hard to leave. He did not have the coping skills or support to navigate it well. Neither did I, but at least when I was there with him, there was some sense of normalcy. Now there was none, nada, zero! My heart was shattered.

I knew I had to rally. I had a new job and a new home and had made a commitment to the people who brought me out to California. So in spite of the overwhelming sadness, I stayed, continuing to believe there was something out here I was meant to discover. I pressed on, hoping that somehow my son would be safe. I prayed that having his son home would be the incentive his dad needed to get help and get better. In time, I learned that the alcohol raged even more out of control in my absence. My son had embarked upon his own perilous journey where his faith and belief in himself would be put to the test time and time again. That story is his to tell when he is ready to share it.

As for me, time passed. I threw myself into my work and frequently spent weekend days in Laguna Beach. One of my absolute favorite places to this day. I connected with my son as often as I could and prayed for him always. I had to keep believing that things would be okay. That kept me going.

One Saturday afternoon, while visiting a little shop in Laguna, I came across a flyer. It was information about a school that had an education program in Spiritual Psychology. Well, I majored in psychology and this sounded like an amazingly perfect combination. I knew when I grabbed that flyer that this was something really important and that I would be going to that school. I very quickly managed to enroll, just before the beginning of their upcoming fall semester. Little did I know then how much that decision would alter the course of my entire life.

The job was going well. My boss was great and really let me run with the position. We went through a bit of a rocky time, however, when I told him I was going to school for my Masters Degree. I was four months into a highly-demanding new job and my boss didn't want anything distracting me from my role. He knew the heavy burden I was bearing in not having my son with me, and he believed the answer was for me to spend my free time making friends and getting a social life outside of work. Engaging in a rigorous scholastic program was definitely not on his agenda. What I saw as a way to expand and blossom, he viewed as a distraction. In spite of his objections, I chose to stay in school.

My creativity began to soar inside and outside of work. The truth is, at the time I began school I had not yet completed my undergraduate degree. A little crazy I know, embarking upon a Masters Program before my undergrad was finished. The University of Santa Monica has a great option which allows you to begin school prior to completing your undergrad. I had a little less than two years worth of coursework to complete, so I decided to begin working on both simultaneously. It was a crazy time, but a good kind of crazy!

It was clear that I wouldn't be able to get all my credits for my undergrad completed in time for officially graduating with my Masters in two years, but I wanted to complete the course work with my class So, I graduated from USM the first time as a Certificate of Completion Student, knowing I would have to redo the second year with a completed undergrad in order to officially be awarded my Masters Degree. As I completed my undergrad, I went on to do another year in a newly developed USM program called CHH. Ultimately I completed my undergrad and redid the second year as a Masters Level student. Four years of schooling but I did it! I ended up being awarded my Masters and Undergrad in the same year!

I learned and grew so much during that time. And while I still loved my job, I was compelled to continue my education, so I enrolled in a Doctorate program in Psychology, and once again embarked upon a rigorous education program. Three years later the girl who had come to California without a degree became a Doctor.

It was clear that it was time to take another leap of faith and leave the career that brought me out to Southern CA. Once again, I moved from the security and comfort of the known and jumped back into the void of the unknown. Relying upon my faith to guide me, and utilizing the insight gained along the way, I opened my own business. I now help others work through their relationship challenges, make solid life choices, and better love one another.

Life has taught me much over the years. I have learned the importance of gratitude, faith, perseverance and making pro-active choices, and, I don't wait quite so long to leap these days!

Jeanne's Take-Away: "One never knows how one choice will impact a life trajectory. Looking back on my life, I marvel at each of the 'leaps of faith' I have taken. I have discovered that when I am spiritually focused, and pay attention to life's secret whisperings, that things just seem to work better. These days I spend my time cultivating my spirituality, loving my incredible son, learning and growing my wonderful relationship with my man, treasuring my friendships, and appreciating and learning from my amazing clients. Bottom line: Trust in the power of love; be grateful; believe in yourself, and take calculated leaps as often as possible!"

A Fight with My Car, Car Keys and My Ego

by Jennifer Rose Aronson

"I work really hard at trying to see the big picture and not getting stuck in ego. I believe we're all put on this planet for a purpose, and we all have a different purpose... When you connect with that love and that compassion, that's when everything unfolds."
--Ellen DeGeneres

So, for little over a week now I have been feeling this intense pressure in my chest. I mean, like I have a three-ton-elephant-standing-on-my-chest pressure. A resistance so agitating and so strong that up until today, I felt I would have been willing to leap off a cliff just to relieve the uncomfortable weight, ...to experience the exhilaration, expansion and freedom sensations of flying and free falling, which accompany my experience of being in the flow and alignment with my Universe, God, Goddess and All That Is.

So, here I am on a Tuesday morning; I go to Walgreen's to pick up foam board which I will use to create a new vision board of my financial prosperity, and then off to the bead shop to buy the supplies I need to create a piece of jewelry, which I was commissioned to create, when my car key gets stuck in the ignition of my car and won't come out, nor will the car start. And I think "Great," as my head hits the steering wheel.

So I call my amazing loving man, who I feel so blessed to be in a relationship with, and lucky for me is a car genius and I ask him what to do. "Jiggle the key and turn the steering wheel back and forth." Is this his answer? I try, and nothing. Frustration mounts and I think, "There's got to be something else I can do. I just want someone else to fix it!"

But I try what he says, frustrated and wanting this problem to just be over. "What else can I do?" I ask him over the speakerphone of my cellular phone after about 5-10 minutes, frustration mounting, arms, hands and fingers sore from turning the steering wheel which feels like twisting a giant gummy rubber band that is about to slingshot right into my eyes.

"Buy some WD40 and AAA," he recommends. "Are you close to home? Can you walk somewhere to buy it?" "I am not. Noooo..." I say through tears. So with frustrated crying and feelings of hopelessness creeping in, I resign to the fact that I may have to ask for help, another thing I have been having resistance around, and spend a good part of my day dealing with a car problem that I never wanted to have to deal with.

Now it should be said that I am a very aware person. I am aware of my processes, of what is going on inside of me, and aware of Spirit and the messages Spirit has for me, a good portion of the time. And while all this is going on my "inner counselor" – my guidance and sense of the world around me – is telling me, "Jennifer, it's not really about the car anyway."

"Yes, I know that," my Higher Self replies calmly, "But what in the hell am I suppose to do?" says the other part that is now officially raging. I acquiesce to the angry voice in my body and head. I slam the car door closed and scream my head off until I can't scream anymore.

And in that moment after the tension is released just a little bit, I begin to listen. And the more I listen, the more I hear from this other aspect of myself, "I don't want it to work, I don't want it to work, I don't want it to work!" Wow, I think. A part of me is super angry. I never knew this. All the resistance I had been having comes into light and it totally makes sense now, along with the awareness and knowing that there are no coincidences.

"The key in the ignition won't release, yet won't start either." It's the story of my life recently. I am like a fish trying to swim upstream. I am fighting – not the fear of changing (I have such a strong desire to grow and change, which I love) – but fighting allowing myself to receive and become the change I so desperately crave. I am resisting the very things I say and intend for myself to have, the things I truly say I want, and the very qualities I am so desperately yearning to experience: Abundance, Grace, Ease, Prosperity, Wholeness, Trust, Support, Love.

I take a moment and share my gratitude for this awareness, and further clarity comes to my mind. I come to understand the resistance itself. It is an aspect of myself; an aspect that truly wants to fail. It truly wants everything to go wrong and it wants to be proven right, so that it can say and justify and wallow in the, "See, I told you so!" mentality. I have never owned this part of myself up until this very moment; a part that I had tried to push away, deny, motivate or pretend that it would say, or be something else and not a part of me. But there it is, my resistance. And I am grateful for it; because as uncomfortable as it is, it also allows me to know the Light of my being. The truth of who I really am: I am not this resistance. And the knowing of what I do want: I really do want to be supported by God.

I am not sure yet how this part will integrate into my being, but I do feel a little bit more ME, having no more resistance against this resistance. And once I came to this awareness, I called my mom, who came and gave such loving support. She took me to my favorite restaurant, which was literally right around the corner, treated me to lunch and asked, "Do you want an ice cream?" And in that moment of being asked that short, sweet, simple sentence, all my resistance washed away...And I felt Supported, I felt Loved, I felt taken care of, I felt God's love pouring through my mother. And the words she said as God's words. "Do you want an ice cream?"

After the best lunch I've had in awhile, we head back to the car, after stopping in a clothing store where I get a compliment on my jewelry – which I created – and receive inquiry about. "The owner is looking for something to add to give his store 'pop' and think he would really like your jewelry. It is definitely something he would like. You do really good work," says the cheery young woman as we are exiting the shop. So I go back and give the rest of my business cards to the woman, who now stands in the doorway totally at ease, and we head on back to the car to try starting it again, or release the key. Either one is good with me.

And as we walk it dawns on me: without the faulty key, I wouldn't have found this store. And I acknowledge, and thank Spirit for that synchronicity, and gratefully say to my mom, "Yep, and that is how it works."

When we got back to the car, I finally noticed that the car wasn't fully in park. Once I discovered a little stone that I had collected some time ago, wedged in there, I was able to unblock the gear box, the gear easily shifted into park, the key released, and the car started as well.

I felt such relief and wondered why I had to go through such drama and suffering. I realized that it was really about me needing to pause, and look at the situation from a new perspective. When I felt balanced, I could see what the situation really was. From there, I was able to look for new solutions.

In reflection of the day and the events that passed, I have a greater understanding that my resistance, in fact, was a wonderful catalyst for change. It was not "being stuck" as I had first thought, but a moment for gestation, where a new connection between myself, Higher Self, mother, my Creative Self-expression, and God and The Universe occurred. It was a moment The Universe gave me to slow down, be gentle with myself, appreciate the Now of the moment and allow myself to be nurtured. For this moment and many others, I am eternally grateful.

And I am happy to report that from the contact I made with the young, cheery woman in the clothing store that day, I now have my jewelry in the front display window of that store! I realized that we are all guided to new possibilities, sometimes through uncomfortable and difficult situations, yet always perfect in its orchestration for learning the exact lessons we are meant to learn. Life definitely has a funny way of coming full circle. Thank You God, Thank You Universe. Thank You Me!

Jennifer's Take-Away "Many months had passed since I looked at my story, and upon doing so I was able to reflect, and give pause for that moment in time and for the person I was when I wrote it. I am able to hold her in love and compassion and see how big that moment in time was for her/me. From it, I could feel that I am not the same person I was, not even in the same paradigm, and by reviewing my story I was able to pause and see just how much growth I have gone through, just how much radiance, and how magnificent a being I Am – and experience myself to be, in all aspects of myself. How my process, journey, growth has been, and continues to be, guided by Source, as well as how much I am living my truth now with a knowing, openness, surrender and wonder I did not possess back then. It can be summed up by the question and a smile: how much better can things get? Feeling so grateful, so blessed, so honored to be living at this time, knowing I AM LOVE. I AM enough, and I AM here doing great things."

Fleeing the Inner-Prison

by Joelene Robinson, M.A., M.S.S., C.Ht.

"Blake said that the body was the soul's prison unless the five senses are fully developed and open. He considered the senses the 'windows of the soul.'"
--Jim Morrison

It was 42 excruciating years. I was on death's door so many times I couldn't count, and that's difficult to admit. The depression I experienced was so dense and intense I was certain it was a life-long curse of family genetics, some really "bad karma" or something incurable. The sadness, despair and hopelessness didn't seem remotely possible to overcome. Yet I'm proud and relieved to say I did.

As a little girl, I didn't understand why my parents were so unhappy, except for one thing. Every time I heard them fighting in the middle of the night my mother said, "I never wanted them, they've ruined my life," and I felt guilty for being alive. I felt that it was "my fault" that my parents were so unhappy, particularly my mother, and that if I were a "good girl" everyone would be happy. More than anything, I felt that "I wasn't enough; if I was, everything would be perfect." I felt sad, confused and worthless. Add to it, I was a very introverted, shy child, so with everything that happened or didn't work out, I began to conclude "I must have done something wrong because it's all my fault" or "I'm not enough" and "there's something wrong with me."

I spent a great deal of time alone and during summer vacations I imagined all of my friends playing and having fun with each other, while I would sit and yearn to play with others, not knowing why I was always left alone. Twelve years of long and excruciating summer vacations. All of my experiences ended with these same conclusions, that I was lacking, deficient and defective. I was in unbearable emotional pain and my obsessive, negative thoughts about myself were completely out of control and I was locked in my inner-prison. These were endless loops that played in my head for many years into my adulthood. They seemed to be my only friends, along with prayers to God to take my life and make it easier for everyone.

My life started to significantly change many years later when one of my mentors, Mary said, "Joelene, you are like an alcoholic in the way you think. Some alcoholics can't even think about a drink or they'll go into the suck-hole of despair. You are like that with your self-deprecating thoughts. You don't have the luxury of a negative thought about yourself." After I picked myself up and dusted myself off from what felt like a harsh but honest sting, I recognized this was an accurate assessment of the extreme self-hatred I had toward myself, and the pervasive limiting beliefs and negative thinking that shaped my existence, or lack thereof.

I believe that first we think a thought, which feeds into our feelings, which motivate our behaviors and then they shape the landscape of our lives. With this in mind, it was clear that my thoughts were toxic and costing me my life, and had to go, but how? This seemed like an impossible task and even more difficult road, uphill!

God knows I had already experienced living a difficult life in an inner-prison. Why would I now begin what seemed like an endless journey of changing my thinking? I knew my life depended on it.

From my professional experiences and education I now know that, until around the age of seven we don't have logic skills and we're like little human sponges. I believed everything that happened in my life meant something very personal about me. I didn't have the skills to make sense of confusing, hurtful things – or even insane things – in my life, so I blamed others and myself. I created stories about myself. I then begin to create coping mechanisms around the "story" that I believed, and I created evidence to support these limiting beliefs. I also began to identify with myself as the one who "did something wrong" or "wasn't enough" or that "there's something wrong with me." Every time I berated, criticized or judged myself, I tore down my self-confidence; self-esteem and I betrayed myself further.

As I began to wake-up I could see how negative and pessimistic I was and how different that was from the people around me who truly exuded fulfillment, joy, possibility and contentment. I could see it was my mind-set about my life, my world and myself that was holding me back. I had a turning point when my younger brother Todd, passed away unexpectedly at the age of 38. I vowed I wouldn't spend another moment in misery.

I began to challenge my thinking about myself. Intentionally and consciously, I began to become aware of the thoughts I was thinking and speaking, that were motivating me and creating my life. I slowly began to shift my thinking from victim to owner consciousness.

At first it seemed like I would never change and it was a painstaking process. Then I began to make it a game; for example, seeing a big, red stop sign in my mind every time my thoughts were self-critical or judgmental.

It took practice, practice and more practice of building my inner-muscles. Then I began to replace the old thoughts with the truth that I was learning about me. At first I felt awkward, as though I was lying to myself. I began to realize over time, that it all was an old-worn out story from long ago, and finally I could put it in adult-perspective.

As I began to talk openly with my mother, I heard how much I misunderstood and misinterpreted as a child, which shaped my adult-perspective. It has been a relief to hear my courageous mother take responsibility for the part she played in the depression and in my childhood.

Now, it's rare when I think self-deprecating thoughts and when I do, I forgive myself for my judgments and then giggle with myself for being so silly. In the past, I would have berated myself for being so stupid.

I now believe that when we're born, we are innately loving, innocent, joyful, peaceful, creative, empathetic, compassionate and fulfilled. We ALL are. That includes me.

I began to immerse myself in this new, conscious language and retrain my thinking from this perspective. I began to consistently remember the "Truth" of who I really am, from my Authentic-Self. I've since dedicated my life to learning and embodying the practical principles and skills to consistently being happy and fulfilled from the inside-out and teaching others to remember, know and live from the Truth of who they truly are.

At this point in my life I can say I am truly consistently joyful, peaceful and have the most fulfilling relationship with myself and dear friends and family. I cherish and am grateful for every moment of my precious life.

Joelene's TakeAway "Realizing the unconscious limiting beliefs is the first step to healing. Then building my positive muscle mind to rewire my thinking allowed me to create the life I truly desire!"

Heart's Desires May Come In Unusual Packages

by Victoria Koutavas

"When you are discontent, you always want more, more, more. Your desire can never be satisfied. But when you practice contentment, you can say to yourself, 'Oh yes - I already have everything that I really need." --Dalai Lama

There were no children born to my mother's side of the family for over 40 years. Part of the problem was there were just too few of us who might have had children. In my immediate family, there is just my younger brother, Dennis, and me. Mom has only one sister, who had one son, my first cousin Spero. I can't tell you what my brother's process was or why he and his second wife decided not to have children, but I can tell you my story.

I married a man who, initially, everyone in my family hated. Beyond the fact that my father and maternal grandmother dreamed I'd marry a Greek man, the man I claimed to love was the antithesis of everything they thought I should marry. He came from a divorced family, was the child of an alcoholic father and an obese mother, he had a high school education and barely made enough money to support himself, let alone a wife and possible family.

I met him at the age of 20, we moved in together when I was 24, married when I was 26 and my gift to myself on my 30th birthday was getting a divorce. It would be easy to say "they told me so." However, it wasn't quite that simple. We had matured together.

He had a good job and was becoming more and more responsible. Who knew after living together for a couple of years, my husband would choose our honeymoon to become physically abusive? By the time we married, my family – even my father and grandmother – had accepted him. They had his background to worry about, but not even they could have predicted he would become an abuser.

From the honeymoon to the separation, I lived on a roller-coaster ride of emotions. Sometimes, I believed things were going to be okay. I would dream of having children and even had their names picked out. Other times, I was heart-sick over what had happened and how a part of my heart had closed up toward my husband, from the first angry assault. The physical abuse occurred several times during the course of our marriage and in retrospect, I have often wondered who that girl was, who decided to live in denial of what was happening around her. Unfortunately, it was years before the self-forgiveness would begin.

Since I never dated much before marriage, after the divorce it was time for exploration. For the first six years the pattern went as follows: I would meet a man, and as the relationship progressed, I would start projecting onto him what I needed, and then begin fantasizing about having children.

As soon as I realized he wasn't going to play the role I set up for him, one of us would end the relationship and I would be devastated. I experienced the deepest depression after my breakup with John, a widower who had an eight-year-old daughter. That was the closest I had come to (what I thought was) the reality of having a family.

The intensity of the pain reflected the culmination of all my failed relationships rolled into one. I walked around like the living dead. Life was bleak and I felt hopeless.

One day, during my painful existence in the dark, my best friend Cheri arrived at my door with a book called *Women Who Run With The Wolves*, by Clarissa Pinkola Estes. She sat me down and literally read me the story of The Little Match Girl. As tears rolled down my face, she told me I reminded her of the little match girl who kept giving away all of her light and, in not keeping any for herself, dies. That day Cheri helped me light the first match in my massive dark cavern. It began as a tiny glimmer of hope, but it was a light, nonetheless. Soon, I found a wonderfully nurturing therapist who helped me build my own identity, separate from the cultural and familial definitions of what a woman's life is "supposed to" look like. Over time I made peace with the fact that birthing or raising a child may not be what I am to do in this lifetime. I also realized I had a choice in how I was going to "hold" that internally: was I going to dwell on what didn't happen, or spend that time being grateful and enjoying all the good things that did happen?

A part of my journey in choosing to look at what was possible, led me to the University of Santa Monica. I graduated with a Master's Degree in Spiritual Psychology. After graduation, I moved from Chicago to the Palm Springs area, as one of my dreams was to live in a warmer climate. Since I had no children and was still single, it was an easy decision. Shortly after I moved, my cousin Spero, who was in his 40's and single, retired from the family business.

One New Year's Eve a friend and I were discussing the type of female we thought Spero might be attracted to, when she blurted out "Angela!" When I found out who Angela was, it was hard to believe I'd met her brother and sister-in-law, but her name had never come up before that moment in time. Little did I know that presenting Spero with Angela's phone number was going to change my life.

Their first date was in January of 2004, and they asked me to be a major part of their bridal party at their wedding in December. When they announced they were pregnant, it seemed the whole family joined me in feeling a hope that had been missing. When they asked me to be their baby's godmother, I was beyond honored. The minute I laid eyes on my goddaughter Lia, my heart doubled in size and grows with each year she is in my life. As if this amount of preciousness was not enough, four years later her sister Andriana was born. They are more than my definition of joy. To say I love them feels inadequate. Words cannot express how gifted I feel when they unquestionably place their trust in me. My prayer now is, "God, help me be the best example to these blessed souls I can be." They are proof that God didn't forget my desire, he just packaged it differently. Lia, my goddaughter, who broke the spell, arrived just shy of my fiftieth birthday.

Victoria's Take-Away "When I stopped looking outside myself for love and the meaning of my life, I found all my answers within. It's so true that our outer world is a reflection of our inner world. Love yourself and God will give you others to love as well."

A Little Boy's Story of Hope, Love & Triumph

by Anne-Marie Arrow, M.A., Life Coach

"Although the world is full of suffering, it is also full of the overcoming of it."
--Helen Keller

A diagnosis of autism should not come as a shock, but for me it did. As a mother of three, I knew Joey was difficult from the time he was a baby. The signs were there. I tried to ignore them until I could no longer hope for things to change.

It didn't take long for our pediatrician to recognize the signs of autism and recommend treatment. Once the diagnosis was confirmed, the journey began. There was no more denying in the future. Hopes and dreams vanished into thin air, only to be replaced by fear and doubt. Would I be able to handle this? What will happen to my child? Will he ever speak? Love is the one constant that remained through all the confusion and difficulties.

Our family life was forever changed. I was scrambling to make things happen. I was fighting a time clock to get services that did not guarantee improvement. I wondered if I could live up to the responsibilities to be the mother my child needed. In my deepest, darkest moments I prayed to God to take this pain away. I prayed for my child to be "normal." Then, I began to bargain. If God could please help my son, I vowed to spend the rest of my life helping others.

My husband could see I was overwhelmed but his approach was very different. He accepted the diagnosis. When he said, "Joey will be okay," I became angry at words that were meant to support and comfort me. How could he know Joey would be all right? Didn't he see my fear? I wanted someone to join me in anger – this anger directed at a disorder that I knew threatened our child's independence. I didn't want to hear promises that could not be kept. I wanted someone to mourn and cry with me. We were out of balance, and tried to hold on to normalcy as much as possible.

There must have been something God liked in my prayer and my promise to be of service. Somehow I was given the strength. Suddenly the right people began to appear in my life. I was on my way to being an advocate for Joey to have the services he needed.

Shorty after diagnosis, we began looking into treatment options for Joey. We attended support groups and talked with other parents. There were so many different opinions – and very strong opinions for treatment of kids on the autism spectrum. Days were filled with speech therapy, occupational therapy and tutors using Applied Behavior Analysis techniques.

I worked alongside the therapists at each and every session. I learned to trust my instinct and intuition in knowing what was right for my son. Joey and I seemed to be able to connect and communicate on a higher, non-verbal level. I knew what he needed and I wasn't afraid to ask for a different approach to his therapy. When Joey turned three, it was time to consider placement in a pre-school classroom setting. For the year and a half since his diagnosis, I had been run ragged. Therapy appointments, running a home-based

Applied Behavior Analysis program, which consisted of tutors coming in and out of my home all day. Not to mention the time needed to take care of other members of my family. There was only so much of me to go around, and it wasn't reaching all the areas of need. But Joey was making progress, therefore, I was hopeful.

The first pre-school class I observed was with children who had speech and language disorders. I saw the children sitting around doing art projects. Then they transitioned to story time and all sat in a circle. I instantly knew that Joey was not ready for this. He could not sit during circle time and pay attention, much less use scissors and cut an art project. He wasn't even able to speak or tell us what he wanted.

The gap seemed so huge, and these were only three-year-olds. I checked out a typical pre-school class with an aide provided to help him. Again, he was not ready for this environment. Lastly, I went to look at the autism classroom. It was in a portable building at the back of the school. The class was very busy with eight autistic children, many non-verbal. The teachers worked patiently with the children, prompting each action and helping with the simplest of tasks. I quickly left, ran to the safety of my car and began to cry. This was so hard. I called my husband and told him Joey would never go to this school.

This was not where I wanted Joey to be, a special education classroom, a portable at the back of the school, a class filled with kids with disabilities. This is not what I wanted for Joey, and yet, I knew in my heart that this was where he needed to be. These kids were like him, he fit in. This was a place he could learn. Joey was one of them and he just belonged.

I never thought that I would be able to look back on these days and feel peace. The class turned out to be the best possible placement for Joey. He was thriving and I was setting up a daily routine. Within a couple of weeks I was able to observe him at school. Each time he would seek out one little boy, Dominic, to hold hands with as they lined up to go outside and play. Joey had chosen a friend! This was the first time he had a real authentic friend. Joey and Dominic didn't care about handicaps. They liked each other and that was all that mattered. With very little communication skills, these two beautiful little souls recognized something in each other and they were buddies. I was happy. THIS was a typical developmental stage, choosing a friend.

When the decision was made for Joey to start kindergarten in a typical school, so many emotions hit me. I was unsure. He was making steady progress and acquiring skills needed to move forward. But he was still a child with autism. Beginning kindergarten was the beginning of new challenges, in the real world, with typical kids.

So many questions swarmed around my head. Was Joey ready for a mainstream classroom? Should I tell parents he had autism. He lagged behind his peers socially and sometimes acted differently. But one incredible gift that he had was his memory. He could learn by rote very quickly, thanks to the hours of practicing in our home-based ABA program. He loved letters and numbers and would spend hours playing his language-builder cards, even after his tutors left for the day.

Joey's gift of reading and memorizing gained him the respect and admiration of his classmates. Most children were just beginning to identify letters and spell their names. The teacher allowed Joey to shine, to the awe of his classmates. His confidence grew and he became the first child to identify 300 words, the classroom goal. I wasn't sure how much to tell parents about Joey. I wanted him to be accepted, but because there were times he acted differently, I wanted people to understand why these seemingly odd behaviors occurred. I didn't want him to be teased.

While I was deciding how much to tell others, a situation occurred, which brought Joey's situation to the attention of parents. Another boy with autism was placed in an adjoining kindergarten classroom. He had many disruptive behaviors. Parents began to talk, and they sought me out with questions. I was asked to speak at a parent meeting and answered many questions about children with autism. I had the knowledge and experience. I understood the concerns of parents. Mixed feelings of gratitude and compassion filled my heart. Joey had "made it" in a classroom, the other little boy had not. I understood the pain that filled his mother's heart.

Now everyone knew that Joey had autism. I would not have chosen that path for him, but I know it set the stage for Joey to fully accept himself, and in doing so, he was embraced and accepted by others. Joey continued to overcome challenges with help of teachers and classmates. In sixth grade I stopped by his school to drop off chocolate chip cookies for him to share with his classmates. It was his birthday and he has been a part of the school for seven years. He was becoming an amazing young man.

Joyfully, I encountered many familiar faces – parents, teachers, therapists, and friends. We were all amazed that Joey was 12 years old. Tears of joy filled my eyes, as often happens at moments like this. Joey had been through so much and always held onto the belief that he was perfect, that he could do anything. When the principal asked him to be a "buddy" to a boy on the autism spectrum and help him navigate the playground, Joey proudly agreed. Joey's charismatic personality and willingness to speak about autism has been an inspiration to many. In 5th grade he chose to do his science project on autism, proudly sharing his presentation with his classmates.

When asked to speak before the California State Assembly, Joey enthusiastically agreed. Joey waited his turn through hours of testimony. Then he finally got the microphone and began to speak. "My name is Joey Arrow and I have autism." He spoke of the importance of therapy, early intervention and respite care for parents. When he was done the assembly chambers broke into applause and a standing ovation.

As Joey walked down the aisles he was high-fived continually. Many staffers in the capital had seen Joey speak on closed circuit TV. As we left the chambers and walked down the hallway we were approached by those who wanted the opportunity to meet Joey and shake his hand.

In our wildest dreams and deepest hopes, we never imagined that Joey would play baseball and be the starting pitcher in his AAA playoff game. We couldn't have hoped that Joey would try out for a power league volleyball team and make it. It would not have seemed possible to dream that he would be invited to train at the US Olympic Training Center with 35 other boys from across the US, chosen from tryouts across America.

Joey is now 13. We will never forget that little boy, who at two years old would take our hand to lead us towards what he wanted. We can't forget the moment his pediatrician sat us down to tell us tests confirmed the diagnoses of both autism and mental retardation. Those memories will always be present and a part of how Joey's journey in life began.

Yes, miracles can happen. Joey's hard work and determination to take on challenges brought much success in his life. I have kept my promise to God and continue to help others who are just receiving this diagnosis. God was with us all along and gave hope to keep on believing.

Anne-Marie's Take-Away "In the midst of pain and confusion it was hard for me to see beyond the daily life challenges. In the end, it was the love, determination and spirit of a small child with a disability that taught me the true power of believing. Through Joey's diagnosis of autism, I discovered how to give up my 'control' and allow God's love to gently guide our lives. With this came surprises and healing that I could never have imagined."

Please Send Me a Billboard!

by Nancy Gex Klifman

"Life is one big road with lots of signs. So when you're riding through the ruts, don't complicate your mind. Flee from hate, mischief and jealousy. Don't bury your thoughts, put your vision to reality. Wake Up and Live!" --Bob Marley

I was in a "bad spot" in my life. Separated from the man I loved and with whom I believed would spend the rest of my life, I had enrolled in a master's degree program in Spiritual Psychology. Like the proverbial phoenix, I was trying to rise from the ashes of a fairytale life that had combusted around me.

We had been married 13 years and had two beautiful daughters, the eldest just approaching the shaky ground of pre-teen. We had two Labrador retrievers, two ponies, a home within walking distance of my children's private school, and a family farm retreat in the country... all of the trappings of a most wonderful life. My husband had recently revealed to me that he was gay and my mind kept trying to rationalize his information, compared to the wonderful man who had been my lover for 13 years. My heart was broken and my dreams of "happily ever after" lay in tatters at my feet. I was raw with pain anger, loss and very, very scared.

Landing at Hobby Airport in Houston, Texas, I was returning from an immersion weekend at the University of Santa Monica where I traveled once a month. During a very emotional counseling trio at USM this weekend, one of my classmates had skillfully guided me through the dark story I was experiencing. Slowly and painfully, I revealed the depth of my despair, and finally shared my horrible feelings of inadequacy as a woman. I cried as I questioned my ability to raise two children with this man I no longer knew. I expressed my doubts that I could ever trust another man. My counselor gently challenged me to keep my heart open to what possibilities Spirit might present me from my perceived experience of loss and sorrow. I had accepted the challenge with a healthy degree of skepticism.

It was past midnight. I was emotionally exhausted from three days of intense study. I always likened my time at USM to going to a "mystery school" where the normal life was suspended. I was driving home from the airport, shifting my internal gears, preparing to re-enter the "real" world. I was anticipating a few hours sleep before waking my daughters to take them to school in the morning. I felt vulnerable at night driving alone on the busy freeways in Houston. I was on my cell phone, checking in with my dear friend Pamela who insisted I call her each month when I landed so she could "talk me home." I warily scanned the early morning traffic. As I glanced up I saw the billboard that read: "Someone You Love is Gay."

My physical reaction was strong, I tasted the bile in my throat, tears sprang to my eyes, my belly clenched and roiled, my chest felt hollow, dry and aching. I burst out to my friend, "Oh no, now I have to love him too!" I clearly saw this as the sign in my life that I was supposed to take very, very personally. Fortunately my friend was clear that this was no accident. She was as surprised as I, but encouraged me to accept the message as a direction. She held the loving space I needed to rant and rave and then come back to the wonder that on this very weekend while I had been away, this billboard had been placed on this freeway for me to see.

This particular billboard campaign, purchased by a local church, ran for three months where I was living and raising my girls. There were few freeways I could drive that didn't echo the message to me. During this same time my mother was extremely ill, hospitalized an hour north of town. I drove often to be with her, easily seeing these billboards three or four times as I worried my way to and from her bedside. The shame I felt each time I saw them was intense. I could feel the sensation in my scalp, like my body was trying to turn inward on itself. I wanted so badly to make my husband the reason for my unhappiness, and to prop myself up with righteous indignation. A woman scorned and left with two little girls to raise alone. This is how my family viewed my situation. I recognized that this billboard campaign was a universal intervention into my experience that only I could interpret.

I could choose to resist and go with what I was being supported to feel by my family, or I could take this message from Spirit to heart. I have no doubt that this media campaign happened at that time and place for the greatest good of all concerned.

I know that it had to hit home for others. Mothers and Dads of children they may not have spoken to for years. Gay people who had chosen to be true to themselves, and how they must have felt the love that was on those signs. Choice was what was offered to anyone who read the sign and it hit viscerally, hard and fast, taking us first by surprise, then asking us, repeatedly, to confront the shame and the fear and become vulnerable once again, to feel the love available to us.

I chose vulnerability. I chose to love and accept my children's father in his new life. I chose empowerment over victim. I chose to love myself and to model love and compassion to my children and my extended family. I once again created a sacred space for their Dad in our lives. I began the work to forgive the judgments that had held me hostage in my misery. I began to heal.

Because Spirit sent me a billboard, a ripple effect occurred. Like the pebble cast into a still pond, from this intervention into my reality, first my children, then my immediate family and then the many, many people I have worked with as a psychotherapist and beyond them, many hundreds of people have benefitted from my clear choice to love my children's father and to not be a victim.

I am happily remarried to a most wonderful man who adores me and accepts and respects my former husband. We have an extended family that includes my children's dad and his partner. We share the joy of our grandchildren together during our family holiday gatherings.

Life is transformed by "billboards." They come in the form of a song on the radio, a message on a tea bag or an unexpected sighting of an animal. You will know when you are being contacted. It will always be in the service of loving. Watch for them, most are more subtle than my billboard!

Nancy's Take-Away "Spirit is always in communication with us. It is up to us to notice and interpret the messages which may seem harsh on the surface, but they are always messages of love."

Coming Out

by Dominique Lelong

"Go confidently in the direction of your dreams.
Live the life you have imagined."
--Henry David Thoreau

I am ready to leave all of you
I am ready to let go of the jail of my ego
Ready to put myself first,
Ready to say no,
Ready to set myself free
As I release my fears from the role that I have played
up until now
I am ready to stand up,
with courage,
with devotion,
with compassion
I am ready to face my own reflection.
Now is my time to follow my heart
Now is my time to be authentic
Now is my time to forgive myself
Now is my time to celebrate all that I am
Time to shine,
time to dream,
time to receive
As I have longed for so long to dare to be me
Now is my time to stand up on my own
In total surrender,
in total acceptance,
in total reverence.
Now is my time to claim my own freedom.
As I let go of all these years of silent torture

I wish to remember forever
How far I have come to say no more.
I am more than my weakness,
more than my failures,
more than my lies and my covering
They all remind me how much
I have dared to get to know me by heart.
I am more than the shadow of my life
I am belonging
to my return of innocence
I am belonging
to the beauty of this world
I am belonging
to the ones that came before me
I am belonging
to my own salvation
Belonging to my life,
Belonging to my self,
Belonging to my soul
I have longed to belong for so long
I have longed to be at peace with who I am
I have longed to just be me
Today I am risking everything,
praying on my knees
As I surrender naked
vulnerable in my own truth
There is no coming back
here and now
There is no coming back
to my old secret
There is no coming back
to protect myself
No coming back alone,
No coming back in tears,
No coming back in fears
As I have failed
again and again

to tell you
The truth
of who I am
There is no coming back
as I am
coming out.

Dominique's Take-Away "This piece is a declaration of independence, of sorts. There have been many aspects of having to let go for me to find myself. Coming out to me means that I dare to realize my dreams, I dare to share the truth of who I am, and I dare to answer my higher calling. Coming out is more of a coming home."

Follow Your Heart

by Deirdre G. Pasky

"Let yourself be silently drawn by the strange pull of what you really love.
It will not lead you astray." — Rumi,

As I unpacked and got ready with the other cheerleaders, I could see the ocean from my dormitory and I wondered what it would be like to attend college here. It was a beautiful day and a beautiful campus. I could feel the warm sunshine on my face as I made my way down the path to the field where the other squads were assembling. I had never heard of Pepperdine University before now. I was intrigued that this amazing school overlooking the Pacific Ocean was just a two-hour drive from the valley where I was attending high school. This made cheerleading camp accessible and affordable to us.

I had just finished my freshman year of high school and made the junior varsity cheerleading squad, and I was ecstatic to be attending summer camp here. I was full of hope and I began to believe good things could come my way. Up until that moment, it was as though I'd been so focused on the immediate path in front of me that I was missing out on the world that was available all around me. It was like someone had tilted my head up so I could see a whole new world, a world of opportunity and inspiration.

I really liked the girls on my cheer squad but often had trouble doing the silly things that other 15-year-olds were doing, like having food fights, talking about who was wearing what, and running through the fountain in the middle of campus to get soaking wet on a hot summer day.

I thought all of that was nonsense. I didn't have time for nonsense. I reluctantly but loyally stayed with my squad as they frolicked about the campus and checked out the grounds. I felt connected to this lovely location and in my own way I did have fun. At that time, I felt most comfortable being present as an objective observer and taking pictures. As I watched them through my camera lens I wondered why it was so hard for *me* to just have fun.

The last time I remembered feeling truly carefree was before my father left us. I deeply missed not having a father, but that didn't have anything to do with me at the time. Or, did it? I was more interested in the job at hand, learning and perfecting our routine for the upcoming competition. I felt lucky to be there, so I believed that doing well would demonstrate my feelings of commitment, or so I thought. You see, this pattern served me well almost all the time, but at others times, it limited me from just being me. I wanted to be the smart girl and the good girl because I believed that would ensure my success.

I cherished my week at Pepperdine's summer camp and eagerly looked forward to my sophomore year at Alhambra high school. I'd made it into one of the popular clubs on campus. I was full of hope and optimism for the future. If this amazing campus had been just an hour and a half from my home all this time, I wondered what else was out there? My whole world was expanding and I knew I was right where I was supposed to be.

Alhambra's football season went smoothly and it seemed to me that being a cheerleader afforded me some luxuries, like being invited to be a part of the various cliques on campus. I was elated and eager to continue connecting with others and to keep on achieving my goals.

The parents of one of the members in our high school service club owned a beautiful vacation home in Lake Arrowhead, with a ski boat, private dock... the whole nine yards! I felt blessed to be able to enjoy such a wonderful vacation there, something my family would not have been able to afford otherwise. I especially enjoyed spring break at the lake because we got to water ski and soak in the sun. This "vacation" house was big enough to fit all of us girls comfortably. My friend's parents were available in case we needed anything, which was really special to me, having lived in a home where parents were rarely ever home. My friend's parents cooked for us when we got hungry. They would take us out on the boat, or out to go shopping. There were also gorgeous teenage boys in the area, who were exhibiting their athletic prowess behind passing ski boats. Although I had my sweet and loving boyfriend Marc at home, I would have seriously considered trading my old life for this new one. The whole experience was in such contrast to what I'd been used to, and it was glorious! Things were going great! How could I've known that it was all about to change?

In April, the following spring, I was devastated to learn that I was pregnant with Marc's baby at just 16 years old. How did I let this happen? Confusion and panic set in, and although I am not opposed to abortion, the thought of having one never entered my mind as an option with this pregnancy. I had plenty of time to consider it and do it. I wasn't sure why, but even at that time I had a deep sense of knowing that I was going to have, and raise this baby.

I wasn't alone, either. Another girl on my squad got pregnant several months earlier, but she chose to have an abortion. She did not openly talk about it then, she simply left school for a few weeks and came back significantly slimmer.

Later, because I was pregnant, she trusted me and confided in me that she did in fact terminate a pregnancy. I was grateful that she trusted me, but it hurt to realize that I had earned her trust only because I was pregnant myself.

Marc, my baby's father, was my high school sweetheart and my first true love. I told him right away that I was pregnant and to my surprise he was very supportive, just one of the many blessings along my path in this life. His reaction to the news was consistent with my experience of him and proved to be unwavering the entire time we were together. He was the embodiment of unconditional love in my world. He was kind, loving, patient, and unbelievably supportive. Marc wanted to get married right away, but I knew I didn't want to get married just because I was pregnant, so we waited.

I decided that I would wait as long as I could before telling anyone else about the pregnancy. The funny thing is, if I could have gone the entire time without "showing" then I would not have told anyone. That made perfect sense to me as a 16-year-old. I was unable to tell my mom because I was devastated, certain that I had let her down. My mom had such high hopes for me, and she frequently voiced her vicarious dreams for my life.

I considered running away to avoid the inevitable, but soon came to my senses and realized that would accomplish nothing. So as I began to "show" at five months, I had no choice but to tell my family. I went to my older sister first to recruit support, and then together we went to my mom. Mom said she already knew because she'd noticed the changes in my petite body already taking place, and had been waiting for me to come to her.

More patience and support came my way, this time from my mother, and I saw it as another blessing on my path in this life! In December, just before Christmas, Marc and I had a healthy baby boy who we named Joshua. He was pure love. Due to the unanticipated conception, after taking such cautious and careful measures, I knew that this child was meant to be. Today, I look back with awe at the knowing I possessed at such a young age

I find it astounding. This child gave me life. This child was my life. This child saved my life. He did in fact keep me anchored to this earth when I contemplated leaving at times. Perhaps he came to help me heal, or perhaps we are healing each other. In any event he is a strong force and profound presence in my life.

Marc and I married ten days after Josh was born. Marc stepped into the roles of husband and father as though it was his sole, and soul purpose. We were his pride and joy. There was nothing he wouldn't do for us. Even so, after being married for about two years, I felt deeply driven toward something else but didn't know what. My soul was missing something and I was willing to sacrifice everything but my child to go and find out what it was. I carried deep feelings of guilt for leaving Marc, who was such a loving husband and father to our son. Both of our families judged me and hated me for leaving Marc. Perhaps that compulsion was my soul drawing me back home to myself.

Over time, I began to revisit my dream, piece by piece. It was through being on my own that my confidence grew, which in turn facilitated a notion that my dream might still be a possibility. My mother instilled in me a strong value for the importance of academics, so that was my vehicle.

Academically, I easily completed my high school requirements and immediately began classes at a community college. I was attempting to get back on my perceived path of upward movement. I spent the next decade working, going to school, and raising Josh. During this time I began to yearn for more of what I'd felt was missing from my life, but all I knew back then was that money and time were scarce. Little did I know, what I needed had little to do with that. Pinching all my pennies allowed me to attend a community college but going to a university would have required a scholarship. Time felt like it moved at a snail's pace during this period and I had to dig deep for patience. Perseverance is all I had; patience would come later. Everything unnecessary had begun to fall away as my focus became clearer. I had to take small baby steps, it's all I had, and it was all that I could do. Eventually I managed to get my AA at the community college level, which meant that I was ready to consider university level.

I applied to several universities with the requirement to be geographically accessible to me as a single mom in southern California, which limited my choices. Every part of me wanted Marc to be in Josh's life, and moving away would have disrupted that. I was proud and happy that Marc and I were able to amicably co-parent Josh. I've always had deep respect for Marc as the father of my son, and couldn't imagine creating a challenge in location for him to continue his "hands-on" fathering. From all my applications to local universities only one granted me acceptance AND offered me a scholarship to attend. That university was Pepperdine!

How could I have known that a decade later, I would return to my place of inspiration with a scholarship to complete the dream that I thought I had lost? Somewhere deep inside flowed the belief that I could experience my dream and I was tapping into that energy flow now.

Deirdre's Take-Away "I learned to embrace the things that inspire and interest me because that is how Universe (Spirit) is guiding me in a Purposeful Life. I learned to release my personal judgments associated with 'feasibility' (time & money) and put my energy into practicing Allowing & Accepting. As I practice this, I've experienced many magical, synchronistic events and I am stepping into a new 'Dreaming Big' way to serve the world. Who am I to stand in the way of Spirit?"

Road Trippin'

by Donna Edwards Goldman, M.A

"Life is a traveling to the edge of knowledge,
then a leap taken."
--D. H. Lawrence

On a beautiful summer morning ten years ago, my two daughters and I, Jenn, eight years old, and Lindsay, six years old, headed off for a grand adventure. The plan was to spend a few weeks sightseeing and driving up the West Coast, culminating in Orca whale watching outside Bellingham, Washington. As a mom, kindergarten teacher, former Girl Scout, and now Girl Scout leader, we were prepared for almost anything. After seeing the elephant seals in southern Big Sur, Cannery Row in Monterey, the boardwalk in Santa Cruz, and San Francisco, we headed to the top of California.

Our destination was Gold Bluffs Beach Campground. I had heard and read that the drive into this campground, through Fern Canyon, was as spectacular as the beach campground itself. Elk freely roamed, and reportedly parts of the film, *Jurassic Park*, were filmed in this canyon. At the top of the road heading down to the campground was a sign saying, "Steep windy road. Vehicles over 24 feet prohibited. Rough dirt road for 8 miles." Being the consummate adventure girl, my first thought was, "Awesome! We're 24 feet. We just made it!"

The drive down was indeed spectacular. Lush, verdant, green moss and ferns lined the 50-foot canyon walls. I felt as though we were driving through an enchanted forest. I fully expected little fairies to be flying around, welcoming us to their Fairy Tale Land. Although the road was steep and slow going, I felt joyous, alive, and free – excited to be going on this adventure and to be sharing my love of travel and adventure with my two precious daughters. At no point did I feel any fear.

After about a 40-minute drive, the road ended, and opened up into a beautiful, windswept beach backed by a lush rainforest. Pure heaven!! We spent the day beachcombing, hiking the Fern Canyon Trail, and trekking through the forest searching for treasures and fairies. Although there were a few other campers, we felt like the beach and the forest were ours alone to explore. We basked in their magic and mystery.

That night, we cooked hot dogs and beans over an open fire, made s'mores, and stayed up far too late singing songs, telling stories, and enjoying the magic of the night sky. It was after midnight when the fire finally died out and we headed off to bed – lulled to sleep by the soothing sound of the waves, and the enchanting chorus of cicadas. We awoke at dawn and began striking our camp. We were excited to cross the border into Oregon. Our next plan was to explore Ashland, Oregon and the Rogue River.

As I was tidying the kitchen and battening down the hatches, I sent the girls outside to shake out our tarp. The words "Shake the tarp out *away* from the fire pit!" had barely left my mouth when I heard a bloodcurdling scream. Although it seemed like an eternity, it only took my brain a second to piece together what had happened.

I looked outside to see Lindsay jumping up and down as though she were on fire. She had fallen backwards into the fire pit into the still burning-hot coals from our late-night fire. As I examined my panicked and writhing daughter, I could see that the coals had burned through her layers of clothing, and had seared to her lower back. I shouted for Jenn to get a bunch of ice from the freezer, as I attempted to peel the layers of clothing off of my terrified, screaming, and burning daughter. At some point, I realized I was peeling layers of skin off with her clothes. So, I lay her face down on the picnic table, and dumped ice on her back. It seemed as though the ice instantly melted, while her back continued to smolder.

Jenn kept running back and forth getting more and more ice. After what felt like an eternity, Lindsay calmed down enough for us to transport her to the back bed of the motor home. Even in my terrified state, I thanked God we had ice. I thanked God for my daughter, Jenn, who played nurse as I did my best to play doctor. Fortunately, we had clean rags. We kept applying handful after handful of ice, and covering it with clean towels. With not another soul around, we quickly loaded the rest of our things, and headed out of camp to seek some medical attention.

God bless both of my precious and extraordinary daughters. My eight-year old daughter, Jenn, seemed to instinctively know what to do to comfort her younger sister. While I drove, and as the cloth on Lindsay's back became warm, Jenn would add more ice and then gently cover her sister's back.

Tears began streaming down my face when I heard Jennifer's precious voice singing to her sister. I looked in the rear view mirror to see her little hand rubbing her sister's hair, comforting, soothing, and nurturing her little sister. Jenn's actions and presence seemed to calm and quiet Lindsay, as she finally settled down and stopped crying and squirming. Many years later, Linds reported that she couldn't hear her sister's singing above her own crying. So she willed herself to stop, so she could hear her sister.

At the top of the road, there was a park ranger. Her strong encouragement for medical treatment was for to head to Portland, or even better Seattle, as there was no decent medical facility for miles around. So off we went on the seven hour drive to Portland, Oregon.

After a while her back was no longer warm to the touch. I felt it was safe enough to dress the wound. I applied two entire tubes of antibiotic, and three large gauze bandages. I knew enough to know that keeping her wound covered with antibacterial ointment and bandages to prevent infection was the most important thing.

It was after midnight when we finally reached Portland. I was surprised and a bit frightened when I discovered a city of bridges. I have a pretty intense fear of heights, and of bridges in particular. There was construction on some of the bridges, which confined us to a very narrow passage across. Navigating this type of situation – especially in a motor home – is among my least favorite of things.

Exhausted, at 2:30 in the morning, with my children peacefully sleeping, I found a safe place to crash for a few hours. I just didn't have the heart to drag us all into the emergency room.

Ironically, or not, my husband at the time, Neil, was on a business trip in Seattle, a mere three hours away. So I decided to get some sleep and head to Seattle the next morning. God, Spirit, The Universe, or whatever one's version of a Higher Power is, was certainly with us throughout this entire journey.

We arrived at my husband's hotel room the next morning. Although I was still fearful and concerned about my daughters back, I was so grateful for the coincidence and synchronicity of the timing of Neil's business trip.

By this time, I had spoken to my daughter's pediatrician. Apparently I had done, "all the right things," and unless her symptoms worsened and showed signs of infection, she didn't see any reason for a hospital visit. She seemed to think Lindsay might be at more risk of infection in the hospital, than where we were in the hotel room.

Lindsay was her own hero. Her dressings needed to be changed often, and it was an excruciatingly painful process. I was grateful for the distraction of the television. I was grateful for my husband's presence. I was grateful for the pharmacy a few blocks away that provided all of our medical supplies. I was grateful for a free place to park our motor home right around the corner from the hotel. The hotel room became our hospital and sanctuary as we nursed and helped to heal Lindsay.

Although this was certainly the most challenging experience our family had ever endured, I was instantly aware of the gifts and the blessings for all involved. I saw and experienced Lindsay's incredible strength of heart. Not once did she ever complain. I learned so much about my daughters and myself on this trip. I discovered the Spiritual Warrior in all of us.

No whining... no complaining... We did what needed to be done, and for the most part, handled ourselves with courage, right action, calmness, thoughtfulness, grace, and respect.

Upon reflection, I can see how we were all touched by Sprit's healing grace on that trip. And although I would never wish this experience on anyone, I am grateful for the many blessings that resulted from such a horrifying experience.

My soon-to-be 17-yr-old daughter, Linds, is now in her junior year of high school. She is coping with the demands & pressures of AP & Honors classes, exploring college options, a boyfriend, and her parents lovingly completing their 24-year marriage. As she navigates her way through this next phase of her life, gratefully, she can draw upon the strength of heart she exhibited during a tremendously challenging and painful time in her life. Then, as now, she can draw upon her courage, resilience, optimism, adventurous spirit, will and humor.

We have explored the possibility of plastic surgery to improve the appearance of the large and wrinkled scar that covers the majority of her lower back. At this point, she is not at all interested. She wears bikinis, and is incredibly open about sharing her scar & her story. For her, I believe, her scar is a visible, tangible reminder of who she is and what she is made of. I think it's like a badge of honor and courage that she carries with her. She does not want to erase that.

Donna's Take-Away "This story is a reminder to me of the extraordinary power of unconditional loving. How Spirit's Healing Grace is present and available at all times. And how even during the most challenging and seemingly insurmountable circumstances, the very best of the Human Spirit can emerge and triumph."

Abuse, Addiction and Salvation

by Judi Larson

"Courage is a kind of salvation." --Plato

I grew up in a home where fear and shame were the most powerful emotions I experienced on a daily basis. My father was an abusive alcoholic. My mother hated herself, her life and also me. Imagine a child five years old, sitting at the breakfast table with her father. The child's father opens up the refrigerator to get milk for their cereal. He realizes there is no milk. He begins to throw things, starts yelling, finds pineapple juice and pours it on the child's cereal. He tells her to shut up and eat. I felt scared, unsafe, and lonely. I felt it must be my fault; I just wanted to hide. What does a young child tell herself when her father, who is to be her protector and keep her safe, screams instead? I told myself adults are not to be trusted, and started living my life and making all my decisions from fear. I knew that if I ever wanted to feel safe I must never share my feelings.

I was always on guard, attempting to make sure I did not make mistakes. If I did not make mistakes, than I could not be hurt. As my life continued I came to realize it was impossible not to make mistakes. This caused me to tell myself there must be something wrong with me. Sure enough, I was right.

I was about six when my parents gave me a little black puppy. I named him Skippy. Skippy became my best friend and he always made me feel important. He went everywhere with me and he slept with me at night. I had finally found someone I could trust. This did not last long however. I was out in my yard one afternoon throwing sticks for Skippy when my father came to talk to me. I will never forget that day as long as I live. My father told me we would be moving to another state and I could not take Skippy with me. My father picked up Skippy, took him with him, and I never saw Skippy again. I cried and I cried. I hated my father at that time. My father told me he did not want to see me cry again or he would give me something to cry about.

From that day forward I attempted to make myself invisible. I did what was asked of me and I stayed out of sight as much as possible. I spent a great deal of time in my room; it felt safe there. I felt like I was a burden, unwanted, and most of all sad and alone. Within a month we were living in a new state. I started my new school and my teacher would take her ruler and hit us across our knuckles when she thought we were not paying attention. This just affirmed what I already knew – adults really do not like kids. I started to become what my parents' friends referred to as a "nice girl." They saw me as a nice girl because I just did what was asked of me and then worked hard at becoming invisible. Sometimes I would sit under the weeping willow tree in my yard. I would dream of riding a magic carpet and I would fly off to a beautiful place where everyone was friendly and I could eat ice cream and play with all my friends. I was not scared when I was in this place. It was hard for me to make friends because we moved six times before I was ten. This gave me even more reason to isolate myself.

I was becoming really depressed. I did not know it was depression at that time. I just knew life did not have any joy. I would cry a lot when I was in my room. My mother was glad when I was in my room because she did not have to spend time with me. There were times when my mother would speak to no one in the house for at least two weeks at a time. Then out of nowhere, she would talk again. I started telling myself it was my fault my mother doesn't talk to me; I must be unlovable. I felt worthless.

I am now going to fast forward to my life at the age of fifteen. My parents were involved a great deal with the Elks Club in the community I lived. This required them to travel out of town some weekends. It was the summer before my senior year in high school. I was in the kitchen baking cookies when I heard the front door open. It was my mother. She told me she had left the convention early because my father was drinking too much and he beat her. She had bruises all over her face. She then told me she was getting a divorce from my father. My father's drinking had caused a great deal of arguments between my parents lately. So when she told me they were getting a divorce, I was thrilled. Now I did not have to lay awake at night wondering when the next fight would happen between them.

My senior year of high school was not the happy experience I expected it to be. I felt like all the kids in my class saw me different because of my parents' divorce. Once again I felt so alone, different from everyone else. Some days I just wished my life would end. I trusted no one and I had no one to confide in when I was scared. Life began to feel hopeless much of the time and I could not see it becoming better any time soon.

Graduation finally happened and my mother moved with her new boyfriend to a new city. She informed me I was moving, also. Great, another move!

The one hope I hung on to, was knowing I was going to attend cosmetology school in the fall. Maybe I would meet new friends that did not know anything about my life. A fresh start! A level of excitement came over me – the first time in a long time I felt I might have a reason to live. School started that fall and I did meet some friends. It did not last long; they always wanted to party on weekends. I did not drink. I was too afraid I would end up like my father – mean and a drunk. No thanks. By the age of eighteen I graduated from cosmetology school. I met the man who would become my husband. I thought by getting married my life would be happy for the first time. I was so excited, on cloud nine for about nine months. Then reality set in. I realized I had married my father; my husband also was an alcoholic. He would have rages and destroy things in the house. Too afraid to be alone, I just put up with my husband's behavior. I spent my time either working or making sure my husband's needs were met.

I was twenty when I became pregnant with my first child. When it was time for the baby to be born I was really scared; this was all new to me. My mother had told me she would stay with me when the baby arrived. Just another let down... my mother did not see my son until he was four years old. When I look back on those years I realize just how empty I really was. I went through the motions of life like a robot – existing but not really living.

When I thought life could not get worse the phone rang. It was my mother. Today was her birthday.

I was just about to tell her happy birthday when she started to tell me the following message: "I have called to inform you I do not want you to ever be involved in my life again." My mom was a really moody individual, so I thought maybe she was having one of those days.

Long story short, I was wrong. I tried to ask her what was going on, but she stated, "You have chosen your life and so have I. Do not attempt contact with me again." And she hung up the phone. I was in shock, numb. I felt rejected, angry, alone, worthless. I was full of shame and guilt; my world fell apart. What had I done to deserve this? I felt hopeless, and felt there must really be something I did wrong to make her mad. I never did get the answers to my questions, because as hard as I tried for years to get her love and approval, it did not happen. The phone call that day was the last time I ever spoke to my mom.

When I look back, it was also the day I started having an eating disorder. I did not know it at the time, but by controlling what I weighed and what I ate, I told myself maybe my mom will love me. I would get on the scale daily, many times a day. Depending on what the scale said, it determined if I could eat that day or not. The scale also determined my self-worth. If I liked the numbers on the scale, I told myself I was ok. If I did not like the numbers on the scale, I told myself I was fat and ugly. Most days I was fat and ugly.

I got into prescription diet pills and had to battle to become free from them. When I could not obtain pills anymore, I became obsessed with every diet on the market. None of this solved anything. I do know I became a prisoner in my own body.

My entire life became consumed with what I weighed and what I ate. I worked hard at being in control of everything in my life. I became a perfectionist, a religious addict, a workaholic. Then the day came when I had become so depressed and could no longer see a reason to live. Hopelessness, anger and bitterness consumed me. In my mind there was no way out but to check out.

A few days later a person from my church, who had been watching me from a distance, approached me and informed me how concerned he was with my depression. In my head I thought, "What do you know about me?" How could he know that the night before, I laid in bed thinking about ending my life? Because I trusted no one, I wondered what he really wanted. But that was the day my journey in life began to turn around. This person believed in me when I did not.

I spent a great deal of time in therapy. I learned to get in touch with my deepest emotions. I want to tell you that my hard work has paid off. I found out through the years of working on myself that I had no identity. When you have no identity, how can you believe in yourself or love yourself? I found out that I needed to live my life from within, and not be looking outside myself to get my happiness. I found what I choose to call higher intelligence. I found the source of love that accepts me unconditionally.

My life today is based on energy. You see we are made of energy and we are connected to everything. Negative emotions are energy in motion, and if my emotions are negative, my energy is low, and I attract all the things in life I do not want. When I continue to look inside myself and live from positive emotion, I attract all the good spirit has for me.

Today I can truly say I love myself. I went to college, and got my degree in social work and addiction. I am currently a successful business owner, making more money than I ever dreamed possible. I have two healthy, adult children, a home and a brand new car. Most of all I have found me, and now live my life for me. I would tell anyone the struggles have made me who I am today. I would not trade me for any one. My life brings me joy and peace of mind. I promise, you can have what I have found, if you want it.

Judi's Take-Away "I realize that everyone matters and is important. There is no precious gift that can compare with learning whom you truly are as a person and living your life from your true self. I know you have come to this earth to complete a purpose. I want to experience what spirit truly has in store for me. It is above anything you could ever imagine, if you just believe."

Awakening to My Life

by Jeff Youngs

"It's exhilarating to be alive in a time of awakening consciousness; it can also be confusing, disorienting, and painful." --Adrienne Rich

I had it all: money, family, successful business, restored Victorian house on Chicago's North Side, and a little red sports car. I was living the dream. My business was doing better than I had ever imagined. It was a stroke of genius, I thought, to bring on the fourth partner, Dave. He could help us get our sales to match the unparalleled capacity and capabilities we had. Eric, John, and I were doing okay; business was good but not great. We knew that we could do so much more. Dave was the perfect fit for us. We had creative and production down cold. In fact, we felt we were better than most. Dave had the salesman's touch. He knew how to identify business and go get it. And he did. Things really took off after that. We shot from $4 million to $10 million within a year or so, and a couple of years later, we were approaching a $13 million year. Then everything changed.

I called a meeting with my partners to develop a vision for our future, but before we got started, John told me that he and Dave had talked, and they didn't want me to be a part of the company anymore. They wanted to buy me out. "We'll use the same formula we used to buy Eric out last year."

How could this happen? What was the point? Things were going great!

A few days later, I was in the office of Bob Wright of The Wright Institute in Chicago. I paid him what I thought was way too much for the hour, and it turned out to be the most valuable, word-for-word conversation that I've likely ever had. I took Bob through my situation. I described to him how angry I was with John and Dave. How difficult it was for me to see them travel to see clients, while I remained back at the office to "hold down the fort." My work had more and more to do with building out the office and buying stamp machines than it did serving clients. I wanted to create a role for myself that had me home more with my family, and as it turns out, I wasn't enjoying what I had created very much.

After describing my situation to Bob, he looked up over his iced tea straw and said, *"I find it fascinating that you could be so miserable in such a marvelous situation!"* BAM!! It was as though someone had hit me over the head with a two-by-four. He had just changed everything. I can't begin to express the impact that his words had on me and the trajectory of my life.

He was absolutely right. I was miserable. I began to see my choices, perhaps for the first time. I looked into the mirror that he held up for me, and I saw a clearer picture of who I really was, than I had ever seen. And I didn't like it. At the same time, I was drawn by the power of this realization and knew in my heart that I needed to know more, and I didn't care how painful it was.

For the first time I could see that it wasn't John or Dave that made my life difficult, I did it myself, and they played right into it. I created an easy opening, and they took it. The truth was that I was not happy. I had felt inadequate and not a part of the team. They went out and sold the work we did, and I stayed back and kept the shop running. Inside, I felt like I wasn't participating and I hated myself for it, and they could see it. I know people only treat you as well as you treat yourself, and I was my own whipping boy. I was miserable, and had been for years. It had just crept up on me so slowly that I didn't recognize it.

I was happy, too. It was a mix that I think many people have. I loved the work; I loved being a "captain of industry." My ego was quite happy with my outer success, and I enjoyed the perks of owning a successful business. All of this was going on inside one person, and that meeting with Wright just made it clear that I wasn't the success inside that I was outside.

Over the next several years, I simultaneously searched to find the truth of "who I am" and did my darnedest to "get back" to where I was. These goals, I would eventually discover, are diametrically opposed.

First step: Sue the bastards! It seemed logical to me; after all, I *did* start the company! I *did* bring them both into the company. The formula they wanted to use to determine the purchase price was no longer relevant, at least in my mind, given the growth of the company!

All that the suit served to do was to torture myself, and my family, with uncertainty and upset over the course of the next year. Although to be honest, it gave me no small satisfaction that I was probably doing the same to them. This all came to a head when we were sitting in the Judge's chambers, nearly a full year after my partners first showed me the door, and the Judge thought it was more fitting to read the *Chicago Sun Times* than to listen to my lawyer's arguments. My lawyer couldn't seem to see what was finally very clear to me: there was no "winning" this thing. Through a series of events that no longer matter, we settled that day for half of what I had originally considered "fair," and what had previously been agreed upon.

John and Dave no doubt considered this a huge victory. But I'm only guessing at that. I don't really know. What I do know is that I was far from "out of the woods." The pay schedule was far less than enough to live on, so I needed to get back to work, and I did, sort of. In one sense I could say that it was "A Long Road Back." But what I have come to understand, is that it isn't really "back." It is forward— just like it has always been.

For the next five years, I tried like hell to "get back." I even started two new agencies and a couple of other partnerships in an effort to re-create the "success" of the past. What I consistently left out in my thinking was this: The "success" in my past that I was trying to re-create involved a large number of variables, only a few of which were under my control.

"I'll do it differently this time," I kept telling myself. What was really happening was this: I could NEVER move forward as long as I was carrying the story of my past with me and attempting to re-create it, only better! That is completely "living in the past." I now know that the only way "back" is forward. Or more accurately, the *only way* is forward.

And forward is where I went. In preparation for my new life and career, I began a Master's Degree program in Spiritual Psychology at the University of Santa Monica. What Bob kicked loose, USM set on a path toward healing and discovery. I reinvented myself. In fact, I think you can safely say that I reinvented myself many times over since leaving my business. Each iteration inspired by something new I learned about myself or how business and the world works.

In my "old" way of being, I was striving to invent myself in the way the world would see as successful, a "One-Time-Thing" that I never quite achieved. In my new way of being, I am ever in a state of change. Growing and "becoming."

My career has had many turns. As of this writing, I still work for myself, and that looks very different today than it did only a year ago. And it all has one thing in common: I am serving people and businesses through clarifying and strengthening communication.

The greatest learning so far is this: I measure success differently. My marriage is stronger than ever, and we've been married 21 years. My kids are all doing great, accomplishing great things and learning to make themselves happy. Each of them is taking great joy in serving others, in their own way. On a recent break from college, my oldest was at home and visiting with her brother and sister. My wife and I came in from running an errand. They were sitting in the living room just talking and sharing with each other. There was laughter and a moment or two of strain, but then back to laughter and warmth. I sat there among them for a time, just enjoying them, and thinking to myself: this is success. I am a very successful man.

Jeff's Take-Away They call it "adversity" when something we call "bad" happens. In my case, I can clearly see that "bad" thing as a gift that awakened me to my life.

Love Lives On

by Ivana Siska

"Death leaves a heartache no one can heal, love leaves a memory no one can steal."
--From an Irish headstone

Some of my fondest memories of childhood are from when I was just around five years old, visiting my grandparents on my mom's side of the family. At the time, we were all living in what was then still called Czechoslovakia. Grandma and Grandpa were old-fashioned, conservative, and hard-working homesteaders. Their property included: a workshop where my Grandpa tooled every possible machine and gizmo necessary; an orchard that bore their fruit and veggies; a barn that housed the livestock, rabbits and chickens; and a very modest two-room home which by then did have electricity and a kitchen sink, but still no indoor toilet – that was in the barn. Essentially, they were poor, and had been for quite some time – ever since the communist party seized all of the familial farmland and forest property that had been their pride and joy, and source of livelihood for generations prior.

My grandparents may have been money-poor, but to me, they represented nothing but the richest and most abundant source of love and spirit I have ever known. I loved them and couldn't wait for the weekly forty-five minute drive that would transport us to the teeny town my grandparents' little home was in.

Our weekend visits were filled with playing outside with my sister and with all the animals, running from the attack rooster, "helping" with the chores, and plenty of spoiling and hugs and kisses from Grandma and Grandpa, but the very, very best memory of all is what happened towards the end of the day.

Dinnertime was super special. Everyone would gather around the table and Grandma would proudly serve all the amazing dishes she spent the entire day making from scratch (and I mean scratch – she raised the chicken, killed it, plucked it, and cooked it), and we would fill our bellies while recounting the day's events. Grandpa was usually cranky and bitter, and would mutter many comments under his breath, but there would always be a twinkle in his eye and a smile on his lips. He would pause, several times during the meal to acknowledge how delicious the food was, especially the soups, and comment on what a wonderful cook my grandma was. She would blush at his words and everyone could feel her pride. Everything was always delicious, made and consumed with love.

As soon as the dishes were cleared, the second part of my favorite times began: the music played and our voices sang. My grandpa was a talented master of numerous musical instruments, and so was my dad. Together, from memory, they would play. Grandma, Mom and my sister and I would sing the songs that make up the soundtrack of my most innocent kinder years. There were hundreds of them; some ancient, some folk, some contemporary, and even some from the top of the top of the music charts in the USA.

The songs we played and sang were a way to communicate feelings and ideas that were difficult, socially daring, or even discouraged politically at the time.

No matter how long I live, the melodies of these songs will forever resonate in my heart because when that music was playing, and our voices were singing, we had our freedom; magic happened. All our aches and pains disappeared, conflicts were resolved, spirits were lifted and the energy of unity and love bounced off the walls and echoed outside into the night for all to enjoy.

These musical evenings were truly delightful. My grandma always teared-up at some selections, and made sure to tell my grandpa how much she loved what he was playing, and they would often serenade each other, looking into one another's eyes knowingly, across that table, in that room, in that little house, in that teeny town.

Looking back at that time, with an adult perspective, I know that I wasn't conscious of their connection, really, nor did I notice that there were really no other physical expressions of caring between them, but I always knew for certain that my grandparents were completely devoted to one another, and eternally in love.

I feel so blessed to have been a witness to what that love looked like, and to have been a part of the connection that they had, and I treasure it deeply. The memory of those weekends at my grandparents' place is even more precious to me because in my sixth year, my dad decided to take our family and escape from Czechoslovakia in search of freedom and opportunity elsewhere. No one knew if we would ever be reunited again. Turns out that we would not sit around that table and sing for another twelve years; memories were all I had.

The passing years were not easy for my family – now living in Canada and struggling to rebuild and support a family from zero – nor for my grandparents, who remained in the home country and suffered the consequences, accusations and fines for being related to someone who left illegally. The pressures of the circumstances were heavy for my parents, and their marriage was not a happy one, but difficult times also pass.

In 1990, post-Velvet Revolution, we were finally allowed to legally return to what was now called the Czech Republic. Once again, we found ourselves, all three generations, sitting around that table, in that room, reconnecting as a family. At this point I was eighteen years old, just out of high school and very sure of myself. My dad had succeeded in moving our family to a place where we had the freedom to live our own lives, our way; and boy, I was doing just that.

Being back in the CR was a humbling experience. I had grown up in a world of abundance, of opportunity, of wealth, and now, sitting in my grandparents' teeny home, I saw the lack. I saw what wasn't, what they didn't have. I saw the hardships that my grandparents had to deal with everyday in contrast to my safe and plentiful life. I saw how hard they worked, how little they earned, how uncertain and fearful they were about the future. I noticed how much they had aged, how frail they had become and how tired they got at the end of the day. I started to pity them and feel sad for them, and then we sat down for dinner.

At dinner, it was as though I was five years old again. Grandma had cooked up a feast and proudly served us huge portions of our favorite comfort foods, and Grandpa complimented her and raved about her cooking.

We devoured the dishes, felt completely nurtured and shared stories around the table, and I caught my grandparents exchanging those loving and supportive looks again.

After dinner, the instruments came out and the musical part of the evening began. My grandfather played the violin so beautifully, and with such energy and emotion, I cried. Somehow the sound of that violin just filled my heart with all the love and comfort only a grandparent could give, and I felt it – all twelve years worth – at once. My grandfather's gift to us was his love, expressed in the only way he knew how: through his music.

That summer visit was the last time I would see my grandma. We received the sad news in Canada, and only my mom was able to fly back for the funeral. My grandma's death left my grandpa alone and lost without his sweetheart of 54 years; he was devastated. He hadn't even gotten the chance to say good-bye to her. He became depressed, his health kept deteriorating, which made him more and more miserable, and soon he had to be moved to a senior home (which he despised).

Five years had passed since I last saw my grandfather, and I found myself back in the Czech Republic, this time working in the film business. I took full advantage of the weekends that I had free and drove through the idyllic Bavarian countryside to visit my grandfather any chance I got. He had aged a lot since Grandma died, and really, he seemed to have lost his will to live.

We spent a couple of hours together during each visit, and each time, he would tell me story after story of his life with my grandma. He missed her so much. They were a "team," he said, getting through many tough times together, always being there for one another.

Now, he had been without her for about 12 years. He was alone, and he wanted to die. The first time he told me that, I was truly saddened and horrified at such a thought. Slowly, after a few visits, and with him telling me stories about his life with Grandma, and about how, without her, he wanted to die and stop being so lonely, I finally understood.

The visits became more and more morose, each time. Grandfather's health was up and down, but his attitude about living was consistently worse. He was crankier than ever, and all he did was complain about everything. Sometimes he would get into such a funk that he would barely speak with me. One day, Grandfather was in a particularly foul mood, and I, ill-equipped to counsel and help, left his room in my own funk and went outside for some air. I found a bench to sit on and I sat there and I cried, feeling pretty sorry for him, for myself, and frankly, angry with the way life unfolds sometimes.

So there I was, seeking some solitude to process all of these deep emotions, and plop, one of the nurses sits down on my bench, completely jarring me out of my state. She was on her smoke break and indulging in what I view as a terribly nasty habit, and she was sitting less than a foot away from me, the smoke from her cigarette wafting toward me and filling my lungs.

I'm annoyed and angry with her and do not make any eye contact, hoping she will be sensitive to my body language and leave. Instead, without looking at me, she starts speaking to me. Was I "the girl from Canada who came to visit the crusty old man with the violin?" she asked. I was so annoyed with her, and the last thing I wanted to do was to have a conversation with a smoking intruder of my personal space.

"Yes," I snapped back at her. She took no heed of my attitude, and said, "I knew your Grandma." That got my attention. This woman, this angel, went on to give me one of the most beautiful gifts of my life.

This nurse happened to be working at the hospital where my grandma had been before she died. She told me that my grandma was in quarantine and was allowed no visitors, not even as she was dying. It was just the way things were done back then. During the time Grandma was in the hospital, my grandfather would visit daily. This was no easy task. He would have to take a bus from his teeny town to the train station, then take a train to another station, transfer to another train, and then take a bus to the neighborhood where the hospital was, and then he'd have to walk the better part of a mile into the hospital grounds to visit Grandma. The nurse told me that he never got access inside, but that he came anyway, and that Grandma knew that he was there. How? Because after that journey, and no matter the weather, Grandfather would stand outside beneath her window, and play his violin. Every piece of music expressed his love for Grandma, his sadness at her illness, and at their separation. The nurse was certain Grandma heard him play because she would smile through her discomfort and after a while, fall asleep peacefully. "And he never knew," the nurse continued. Because of his cranky behavior at the nursing home, she had never felt comfortable enough to talk to him about this, but she would hear him cry at night, praying for death to take him to Grandma, and that the only thing that would sometimes calm him was to have his violin. He loved that violin, but no one had heard him play for years. The nurse and I were both crying huge tears at this point, and I hugged and thanked her.

The next time I returned to visit my grandfather, I had a new understanding, and an even greater appreciation of him. Our visit began with his criticisms and complaints, but then I changed the course of events: I asked him to play the violin for me. At first he lied and told me that he no longer had it, and then, that he never wanted to see it or play it again. I pushed him and pleaded and he flatly refused.

"Grandma heard you," I said. The room fell silent, neither one of us said anything for a long, long time. Rivers of tears flowed. I had never seen my Grandfather cry before, and I'm not sure he had ever done so before. After a long time, he nodded to me, smiled and said, "I loved her so much." He paused and said, "I'll play for you both." And he did. And I felt his love, his sorrow, his essence flow through the music, and wash over me; just like Grandma had. And I was five years old again. Love lives on.

Ivana's Take-Away "What I have learned from this story is that life is full of wondrous events that we often overlook in the moment, but see and feel the value and richness of at a much later time. Love is such a wonder. The connection, contribution and value of love may be intangible, but the effect it leaves is indisputable."

Letting Go and Living With Trust and Love

by Beverly Lubin

"Nothing in the Universe can stop you from letting go
and starting over."
--Guy Finley

One sunny day not all that long ago, I sat on the floor in my 1920's high-ceilinged apartment in the mid-Wilshire area of Los Angeles. I looked around and thought to myself, "Is this it? Am I going to spend the rest of my life here, living to pay rent and make car payments? Am I going to die here?" The possibility of the answer being "yes," the probability of it, scared me, really scared me. But the fact that I was asking was a good sign because it meant I was ready to say NO in a big way. It was just a matter of figuring out how.

How does one get away, drop everything, and change one's life, when that one is a 67 year-old retiree on a limited budget, savings having been depleted by illness and trips to Hawaii? Over the past year, my psychotherapy client list had dwindled and my husband Mark and I were just making it financially. I was feeling stuck.

For sure, Mark was doing better than I. An actor, he had spent the past year in a wonderful play. The play was a smash, well-received by critics, enthusiastic fan base; but somehow it didn't make enough money to keep it going. Not much else was on his horizon except teaching gigs.

I shared my thoughts with him. I was in a rut and though he didn't feel the same way at all, he listened. What can we do to goose up our lives? I longed for new experiences and for excitement while I could still enjoy it.

In truth, this longing had been building for a few years. To begin with, I was diagnosed with cancer in the fall of 2007. Happily, standard treatment of chemo and radiation did the trick and I've been healthy since. But for six months getting through treatment was my sole focus. After the treatment, it was healing, on all levels.

One blessing from such a scary experience is that it forces you – absolutely pushes right up in your face and commands you – to look at your life, to reassess and to be very honest, and to know to the core that at any moment, life can be taken away, or altered irreparably. You get hit upside the head and boom, it's over! Everything you knew, thought was important, thought you needed – it all gets washed away in a single sentence: "you have lymphoma." Beliefs, interests, attitudes, concepts – whatever has been the construct of your life until then – is demolished, and suddenly you're living a new paradigm, one for which you are neither prepared nor want. You don't want this! But it's here, in your face, and you have no choice but to address it. And learn from it. Because if you don't learn from it, then what is its purpose? The cancer experience kicked me into high gear to live life consciously. Who knew how much quality time I had left?

In truth, my journey to "live life consciously" started long before the cancer. Throughout my adult life I had been on a kind of quest to overcome what I believed to be personal limitation, and to live a life of greater mastery and self-expression.

At the time of the diagnosis, in fact, Mark and I were members of a Mastermind Group, a small but intense and committed group that continues to meet regularly to hold us to our potential. Our conversations with Shellie and Leslie were probably the biggest factor in helping me believe I could actually create and survive a radical life change.

So there I was, recovering from cancer, grateful for a nice psychotherapy practice, and feeling like I was beginning my life anew. Cool. Then, after a year or so, I started getting itchy. Okay, so I was getting back my health (thank God!) and life was proceeding nicely. But then the movie *Up* came out and extolled "adventure is out there!" Yes! It is, and I want it! Then came *Under the Tuscan Sky* and I longed to revisit Italy, perhaps to live there, just like Diane Lane had in the movie. And then came *Eat, Pray, Love.* I read the book and realized she was living a life that I want! Then the movie just rubbed it in - how mundane my life was becoming – and, more cruelly, how limited I saw my possibilities to be. Closer to home, friends were taking fabulous trips, and again I would think, "They're living my life!"

The door magically opened for us when we were told the play would be going first to the New York Music Festival, and then onto the Edinburgh Fringe Festival for the month of August. Mark would be away for seven weeks, and I was not about to be left behind. So we talked. We thought. We weighed options. And with little hesitation, we both agreed we would pack up, pick up and move on. What that actually meant, in practical terms, was to be discovered anew, daily.

You cannot imagine, unless you've actually done it, how stressful it is to divest yourself of your life. There are a million questions and a million more details, and the answers only come in dribbles, and only if you're listening real hard. Before Mark left for New York, we talked about what needed to be done and spent a lot of time strategizing. We didn't know how long we'd be gone, so we couldn't sublet; we had to leave the apartment. We knew we had to sell as much as we could in order to pay for the travels, so one of the first things we did was host an estate sale. We invited friends to buy our stuff. After all, if we're going to get rid of things, I'd prefer they go to friends rather than strangers.

I found someone to take over my office and sold the office furniture. What I didn't sell, I moved to the apartment for the estate sale. Our friend Leslie came over. She was crucial in getting us started in the clearing out process. "With each item, think if it has sentimental value and you want to keep it, if it is useful and you want to keep it, or if neither, it goes in a maybe pile or a toss pile." At first I agonized over each piece. In reality, almost everything we owned had some sentimental value; given to us by a friend, or a deceased relative. Dishes are grandmas. The crystal candle holders are from our friends downstairs. But the hardest were the pictures. Years and years of trips and events, visual reminders of a life of joy, relationship, humor. It was awful! Well, at first it was awful. Then something clicked and I got into it and tossed and tossed. I didn't feel "lighter" as some suggested I might. At that point, I could hardly feel at all, I was on automatic, doing what I needed to do.

I spent days going through things and making these decisions. I was focused and obsessed, and thought of little else. As the estate sale day approached, we priced all our items, borrowed clothing racks, and organized the apartment. We set out books and DVDs and videos, and the friends came. It was a party, great to see people, and wonderful to share this experience. Our friends truly showed up for us and were truly generous. At the end of the day we were almost $4,000 richer. What we didn't sell we donated, gave away or sold at a yard sale a few weeks later.

Meanwhile, Mark was in town for just another month and spent much of his time on the computer, arranging to make our lives virtual, sell his car and try to live a normal life. I stressed each time I thought about all there was yet to do. Mark kept saying things like, "Don't worry, it will all get done." Yeah, it will, but you're leaving in a few days and I'm stuck here with a million details!

Then there were my clients. Telling them I was leaving, that I did not know for how long or when and if I would return, was one of the hardest and saddest things I had to do. The therapy bond is deeply meaningful and intense, cultivated and nurtured over time. Though I told them of my plans in plenty of time for us to process this separation, the pain of it was clearly felt by us all. Each time I said goodbye and shared a final hug, I cried big tears, feeling as though some part of me had been ripped away. I often think about those amazing people, and hope they are living lives of fulfillment and joy.

Now, as I write this, I cannot even imagine all there was to do and how I did it all. What I remember is that this was the most stressful couple of months of my life. A myriad details, things to be taken care of, people to contact, doctors to visit, online presence to be expanded, getting rid of stuff and finding places for it, selling the car. Now, from a distance, it's all a blur. I have to re-read my blog posts to really get a sense of the intensity of detail! What I do remember is being very sad, very stressed and generally miserable. It was torture!

Shortly after Mark left for New York, my friend Fredda came from Chicago to help me sort "the stuff" and tie loose ends. She stayed with me for a few weeks, and I think I owe her my life! Honestly. And all the while I was clearing out my possessions, emptying my home, it felt like my life was disappearing. What I knew to be my life was quickly going bye-bye, and I was suddenly a person with no home, in the midst of chaos and demolition. Whoever I was, had to be identified by something other than home, or things, or job, because they hardly existed anymore, certainly not in the way that they had. The stuff was transforming along with me.

We had a yard sale and once that was over, Fredda left and I collapsed. I was exhausted, spent physically and emotionally. The very last day, I sat in the living room, in the midst of what were still too many loose ends, crying despondently. I called a couple of people to help me gather the remaining stuff, practically begged, but no one came. Finally, I paid movers to help me remove the last remains of my life on Mansfield Avenue. I walked the rooms for the last time.

As I closed the door on what, for so many years, had been our home, our place of refuge and joy, I noticed how little nostalgia I felt. Rather, it was with a sense of relief and knowledge that the hardest part was over, that I took that last walk down the hall, out the door, and into the next chapter.

People offered me places to stay. Our friend Kate agreed to take our mail. I sold the car at Car Max. In a couple of weeks, I was gone, first to Detroit to see family and friends, and then on to Edinburgh, Scotland to begin my new adventure, to fulfill the dream. The dream lasted ten glorious months. We traveled through Scotland, England and Amsterdam, then New York, the Midwest, Texas and back to Los Angeles.

I am certain I could not have survived this challenging and frightening experience without my good friends. They helped me stay focused, calmed me and supported this move. On the other hand, I did have some personal skills; skills I had been cultivating for years: staying focused and in the moment; focusing on what is working rather than what is not working; being grateful and appreciative for what I had and what was working; being grateful for my health; trusting that all is well and will be well; trusting in the support and love of the universe; taking care of myself physically, especially breathing! I often meditated and saw clearly the desired outcomes of my move. I was excited about the possibilities, and lived in the excitement rather than the fear. And both Mark and I began to really see ourselves as creative source energy (as Abraham/Esther Hicks defines it), knowing that if we see it and believe it, it will happen.

And these beliefs carried us through the entire trip. Our survival depended on our ability to create and manifest whatever we needed. Place to stay? Spirit says, "Sure." More money? Spirit says, "Sure." Things and people came forward magically to guide us and love us on our way. I've never before experienced anything like it! It was magical, and as one friend put it, "our feet never touched the ground."

This is the way we strive to live our lives now, trusting in Spirit's support and love – and knowing, absolutely knowing, that whatever we need and want will come forward for us. All we need to do is stay positive and clear. Isn't that grand!

Beverly's Take-Away "When I live from the heart and trust in myself and in the Universe, the Universe will provide. When I am clear on what is wanted, am patient, and open to the gifts, they appear, and don't always look the way I imagined!" For my husband, it's "You don't need to have anything, to do what you want to do. Just go do it, and what you need will come forward." Life is good!

Never Give Up

by Alexia Roberts

"Never give up, for that is just the place and time that the tide will turn." --Harriet Beecher Stowe

I was 38 when I felt healthy for the first time in 16 years! It was a miracle! Even though the journey to wellness was a long one, I learned so much and grew exponentially.

My journey started when I was around 22 years old. I started feeling extremely fatigued, became very sensitive to sound and light, gained about 30 pounds and had digestive problems. I was a teacher's assistant in a pre-school at the time. I LOVED my job! Getting to be with children every day was such a joy. I was heartbroken when I had to quit due to being so ill. I grew up with a very spiritual background and felt more comfortable with alternative medicine, but I chose to start with going to western doctors, taking all the tests, only to be told there was nothing wrong with me. I then went to homeopathic practitioners and alternative doctors. They said I had Candida so I went on a Candida diet. NOT FUN! I would feel better for a while, but sure enough the symptoms would come back. I was told it could be chronic fatigue syndrome and that nothing could be done. Over time my symptoms got worse. I started having horrible pain all over my body. It was a pain that was very difficult to describe; it felt like my nerves were hurting. The fatigue became so bad that taking a shower or even brushing my teeth seemed overwhelming.

Somehow I still worked full-time, having various jobs. Throughout the years I tried everything including Hypnosis, Acupuncture, Therapy, Herbs, Energy healings, drinking Chinese herbs (which I wouldn't wish upon anyone) and various diets, just to name a few. Nothing was helping and I kept being told by the Western doctors that it was just "in my head." I was so frustrated! The "illness" got so bad that it was debilitating. I spent most of my time in bed or on my couch and being isolated. I became very depressed and felt that this was no way to live. I became suicidal. I was in so much pain! It was unbearable physically and emotionally!

The fatigue and isolation just got to be too much. I didn't want to live like this. And not finding any answers after everything I'd been through felt so unfair. At times I felt crazy and asked myself, "Is this really in my head?" What was also really frustrating is that I didn't "look" sick. And I became very good at not showing how awful I felt because if I did, nobody would want to be around me, and I wouldn't blame them. I had a war going on inside of me. My spiritual aspect was trying to see the bigger picture. Why was this happening? What did I need to learn from this? But my human aspect felt exhausted, wanted to just give up and felt like it was cruel to be putting me through this. I also had the awareness that there were people out there who were in far more dire conditions. What right did I have to want to give up and kill myself? And there was this little voice, barely audible, telling me that I had so much to offer; that I was blessed with so many things and that it would be such a waste to throw that all away. So it was this little voice, my precious mother, and beloved friends that got me through these dark times. I kept going, not giving up and holding on with all of my might to the belief that I could overcome this.

I think it was around 2004 when I was finally diagnosed with Fibromyalgia. I was 33 years old. At that time hardly anyone had heard of it. I was told there was no cure. It was a friend's mother who helped me get diagnosed. She had gone to a doctor who diagnosed her, and had a medication that was helping her to live a normal life. I finally had some hope! So I went to him and tried the medication. The medication ended up making my muscles spasm, especially my neck. For a couple of days I could barely move and was in excruciating pain. I ended up in the emergency room! It took a couple of days for my body to get back to normal. So that was the end of that. I was so disappointed! On one hand it was a relief to finally know what was wrong with me, but now what? This illness was so new nobody knew how to deal with it. I continued trying different things to no avail.

I've always been fascinated with the timing of things. I don't believe in coincidences. I believe everything happens for a reason. I think about how every moment in my life could be connecting me to my future path. So In 2005, I decided to take a huge leap of faith and apply to a spiritual psychology masters program. I got in! It was a leap of faith both financially and physically. It was an intense program in every way for two years. It was the best decision I've ever made!!!! It changed my life in so many ways and unbeknownst to me, ended up saving my life.

I attended this program with a dear friend of mine named Stephanie. We went through the whole thing together and graduated in 2007. I was so proud!!! In 2008 Stephanie called me one day to tell me about this group that she was recently a part of. After she described it, I recognized the idea because years ago another dear friend had wanted me to join a similar group, but I wasn't ready.

This time when I listened to Stephanie describe this group, everything in me knew I had to join. It was another huge leap of faith financially! It was called a prosperity circle. It started out with seven people and ended up with 15 when the circle closed. It was a group that included people from around the world. And because Stephanie and I had just graduated from our school, a lot of past and present alumni were in the group. We had a conference call once a week. This circle was sacred and each person involved treated it as such. These people became like family to me. It was a safe space to be vulnerable because everyone was there to love, support and uplift each other. So I felt very comfortable sharing about my illness and what it was doing to me, openly crying and sharing my pain.

One of the women in my group met a lady who had my illness and said she had just cured herself of it. So my friend immediately called me and gave me the information. It was the name and number for a lady that worked specifically with Fibromyalgia. I called her and had a long conversation with her. I was very impressed, but when she told me how much she charged I almost had a heart attack! I didn't have that kind of money! I thought it sounded too good to be true anyway, so between that and the money, it probably wasn't going to happen.

But I kept thinking about it and something in me knew I couldn't give up. One of the purposes of the prosperity circle was to end up making a significant amount of money when the circle closed, and I believed with all of my heart that this would happen. However, there was no time line when I would receive this money, but I had faith. So I decided to make an appointment and charge the amount on my credit card, trusting that I could pay it off when I received the "gift" of money.

My one appointment lasted ten hours! At the end she told me I wouldn't need to come back and that I could expect to start feeling better, but she couldn't tell me when because everyone was different. I still had my doubts, AND my faith.

I think it was about three months later when I realized I was actually feeling better! It was a gradual process, nothing dramatic like I had heard some people experience. By the fourth or fifth month I was healthy!! It was amazing and hard to believe all at the same time. I was so happy and joyful, but scared to really believe it was happening. What if it came back like all the other times? I really had to work through the fear and step into the belief that I had released this illness. It was no longer needed and I could say goodbye.

Words cannot express how grateful I am for my health! I am eternally grateful to the woman who helped me release the illness! I am grateful for my family and friends who loved and supported me throughout my journey. I am grateful for everything that I learned: patience, self-love, self-care, persistence, courage, trusting in myself and my intuition, receiving on all levels, keeping my faith and NEVER GIVING UP!

Alexia's Take-Away "The lessons I learned were to NEVER GIVE UP and to believe that ANYTHING IS POSSIBLE! I had an overwhelming feeling of gratitude while writing it for my journey, spirit, my beloveds and for myself. I'm proud of myself for turning IMPOSSIBLE into I'M POSSIBLE!"

Despair Transformed

By Nancy Gex Klifman

Cantilevered out
over the abyss
I look down
and see darkness
The pit of my stomach
fills with sour
somersaults and
I gasp for breath.
Sunlight strikes the
back of my head
and I turn my
gaze upward
Reflections of hope
Shine on my
open face
And I feel my chest relax.

Nancy's Take-Away "Allowing the natural shift of energy is essential. Resistance creates tension, with acceptance the delicious flow of life resumes."

Epilogue

"If you live long enough, you'll make mistakes. But if you learn from them, you'll be a better person. It's how you handle adversity, not how it affects you. The main thing is never quit, never quit, never quit."
--William J. Clinton

"Keep On Believing" is the message that we want to pass on through these stories. There are many challenges we face in our lives. Knowing that you are not alone and have a reason to hope for something better is essential. When you find a message in a story, share it with someone else. You never know who needs that message. When life offers you lemons, make lemonade. We get lessons in many forms, and from each person in our lives. Look for the lesson and pay attention to each message you receive.

Once you get the message, you don't need to get the lesson again. Take time to be still and listen to your inner wisdom. Journal daily and look for patterns. Einstein said, "To continue doing the same thing and expecting different results is insanity." It's important that you are willing to create new results by doing different things. What you resist persists!

Think about what results you really want. Once you do, then paint the picture of what your life will be when you have those new results. Life reflects your inner thoughts and subconscious programming. Be open to having what you really want. Keep your focus on that and soon you will see new results.

As demonstrated in these stories, life does work out and tragedy can turn into triumph. It's all about your attitude. Look for the silver lining and keep on believing!

Wishing you a life filled with wonders!
--John Seeley M.A.
Best-selling Author of *Get Unstuck! The Simple Guide to Restart Your Life*, and *Get Unstuck for Kids! A Fun, Interactive Guide to Empower Your Child for Life*.

For more information go to
www.johnseeleyma.com

Contact us

949 645-5100

Blue Moon Wonders
4492 Camino de la Plaza Ste. 564
San Diego, CA 92173

or email info@johnseeleyma.com

sponsors@keeponbelieving.com

www.johnseeleyma.com

www.keeponbelieving.com

Other books and programs by John Seeley M.A.

Get Unstuck! The Simple Guide to Restart Your Life
Get Unstuck! The Companion Workbook
Liberate! La Guia Sencilla Para Reiniciar Tu Vida
Get Unstuck for Kids! A Fun Interactive Guide to
Empower Your Child for Life

Who Is the One for Me? Audio program
Relationships - Audio program
How to Understand and Communicate with Men and
Make Love Work

www.ingramcontent.com/pod-product-compliance
Lightning Source LLC
Chambersburg PA
CBHW070801100426
42742CB00012B/2213

* 9 7 8 0 9 7 6 5 9 4 2 3 9 *